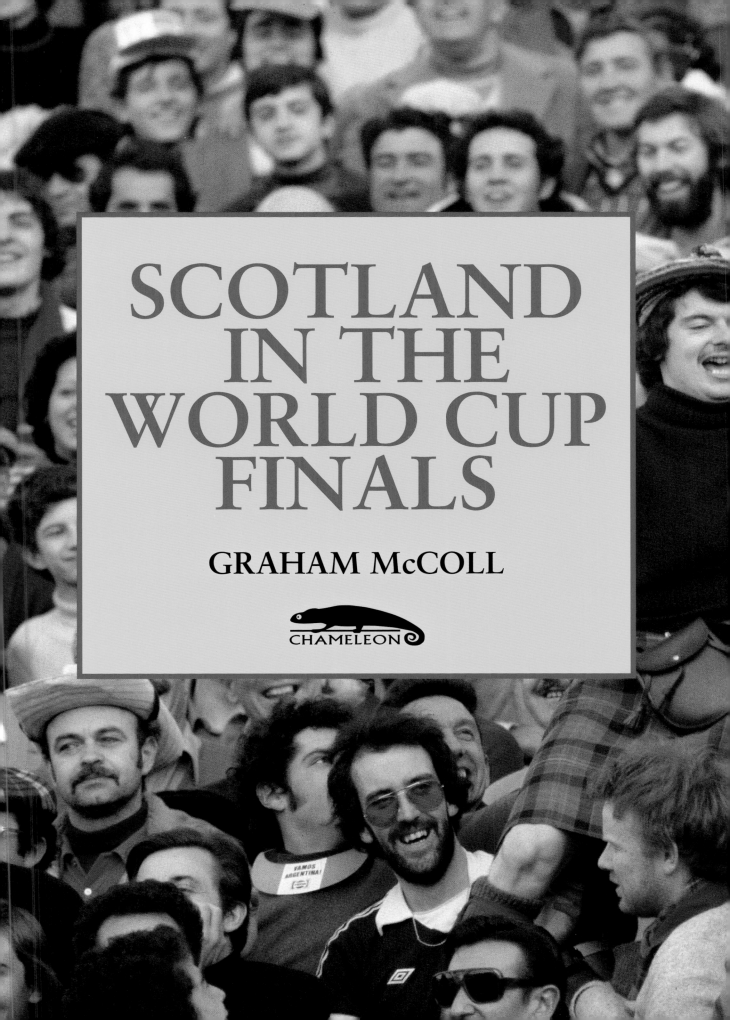

SCOTLAND IN THE WORLD CUP FINALS

GRAHAM McCOLL

CHAMELEON

AUTHOR ACKNOWLEDGEMENTS

I would like to thank Nicky Paris at André Deutsch for all her hard work in putting this book together and for having faith in the project from the outset. I would also like to thank Joe Jordan for his foreword, Iain Thomas for reading the manuscript for writing style, my father for his help with the 1950s pictures, Bela Cuhna, copy editor, and Andy Mitchell at the Scottish Football Association for checking the factual accuracy of the manuscript.

The newspaper archive at the Mitchell Library, Glasgow, was, as ever, a pleasant place in which to pore over the past. For this book, back issues of the _Glasgow Herald_, the _Daily Record_, the _Scotsman_, _The Times_, the _Guardian_, the _Sunday Mail_ and the _Observer_ were invaluable. I would also like to thank everyone else who helped me with this book - they know who they are.

First published in Great Britain in 1998 by Chameleon Books
An imprint of André Deutsch Ltd
76 Dean Street
London W1V 5HA
www.vci.co.uk

André Deutsch is a VCI plc company

Published in association with
The Memorabilia Pack Company
16 Forth Street
Edinburgh EH1 3LH

Text copyright © André Deutsch Ltd 1998

The right of Graham McColl to be identified as the author of this work has been asserted by him in accordance with the Copyright, Designs and Patents Act, 1988

1 3 5 7 9 10 8 6 4 2

Printed in Hong Kong by Dah Hua Printing Press Co. Ltd

A catalogue record for this book is available from the British Library

ISBN 0 233 99330 4

Cover design by Words and Pictures
Pages designed by Don Macpherson

The Memorabilia Pack Company would like to thank the following for their assistance:
Ally MacLeod, Andy Roxburgh, Craig Brown, Scottish Football Association, Daily Record, Edinburgh Evening News, Craig Levein, Keith Anderson, John Johnston, Stuart Marshall, Ronnie McDevitt and Jim Pace.

Joe Jordan's writer's fee for the foreword to this book has been donated to the National Society for the Prevention of Cruelty to Children,at his request.

FOREWORD

By JOE JORDAN

Playing football is a buzz. Scoring goals is such a buzz. Scoring goals and playing football at World Cup level takes your breath away. Ever since I was a boy I had wanted to go and play in a tournament in another country. I thoroughly enjoyed it every time. The centre-halves were a problem but the actual occasion was never a daunting challenge – it was a great thing to look forward to.

In 1973, when we beat Czechoslovakia to qualify, I was just 21. Maybe due to my age I didn't really understand the significance of Scotland qualifying for the World Cup but there was such a gap between then and Scotland's previous qualification that it created a powerful feeling within Scotland. World-class players like Billy Bremner and Denis Law had been part of teams that had never made it to the finals before so it was all the sweeter for them and I could see how much it meant to them. Since 1973, Scotland's success in qualification has been remarkable but that night there were incredible scenes of jubilation and joy. The reaction of 100,000 people at Hampden and everyone else at home after the whistle created a fantastic feeling and that era, that time, that period, that was Hampden at its best.

It was a great time because people lived for their football, not only for their club but for their country as well. I was at Leeds United at the time. The following morning we got to training a wee bit late but Billy especially wanted to get there as early as possible to make sure that the English lads knew that we had qualified – just in case they'd missed it. He reminded them – in more than a few words. We lived in the glory of the moment that morning.

Qualification games are one thing but then you've got to go there and prove it on the big stage. You have the chance to prove you're a world-class player and it is the biggest challenge you'll ever get. Your performance against the best players in the best setting shows whether you have succeeded as an individual and as a team. You don't need to shoot your mouth off – all you've got to do is go and play. And people will assess you and be critical of you or give you pats on the back.

In the 1974 finals none of the teams in our section – Zaire, Yugoslavia or Brazil – were better than Scotland that summer but we lacked experience and knowledge. For me, that's the best Scotland team I played in. We should have done better but there's nothing really to make up for experience. I remember dominating the games but sometimes these group matches get very clinical. And sometimes the experience we have gained being knocked out hasn't really been put to use in the next tournament.

In 1977, we were a good team but in football a year is a long time and when it got to 1978 maybe the team wasn't quite as strong but we should have qualified from our section. In 1974 I'd say there was an element of bad luck; in 1978 I wouldn't say it was bad luck. I think we got such a shock against Peru that it took the wind out of our sails. Then the Iran game was maybe the strangest international game that I ever played in. The whole thing was dead and we failed to raise the tempo enough to win the game. We did very well against Holland but it was too little too late.

Spain in 1982 was unusual. There were thousands of Scots there, as always, but because we were based in a holiday venue the punters saw the World Cup and also had a holiday and got to bring their families out. It was a real festive atmosphere. Again we should have done better. It was a tough group but conceding goals against New Zealand put us under pressure right away. I think it's important to get a good result in your first game because it takes the pressure off. You've given yourself a good foundation.

We were reasonably successful during my time as a Scotland player; we had some good teams and some good players. Hampden was part of that. It has changed now, for the better in some ways, but to have 100,000 people in there creating the Hampden roar was fantastic. I think Scotland have got a lot to be thankful for for the Hampden roar because it helped to get us to a number of World Cups. To play in a Scotland team at Hampden was such a lift. Scotland very rarely lost there, very rarely dropped points. I was delighted to be able to have a part in that and I'm glad I played in that era.

I think Scottish football is about the supporters. Thousands of them gave us a memorable send off at Hampden the day we were leaving for Argentina. Even if there had been no event organized at Hampden, people would have come out and bade you a good journey in their thousands by lining the roads to Prestwick airport, as people did anyway. The Scottish fans have a right to think that they are something special. We had a reputation for causing a wee bit of bother many, many many years ago. I think that has long gone and that is a credit to the outstanding support that we have as a nation. I'm proud to have played for Scotland – it was the highlight of my career – and when I see our players getting ready for the World Cup finals I wish it was me. There's nothing to beat it.

CONTENTS

INTRODUCTION

Jules Rimet, the visionary Frenchman who shaped the reality of the World Cup dream, died shortly after Scotland had first competed in the finals of the tournament. It's likely, however, that Rimet would have approved of the overall contribution that has been made to the competition by the Scots. In the history of the World Cup, the Scottish players have extended themselves far beyond their reach to provide a special niche for their country.

Since 1954, when Scotland first appeared in the finals, their record of coming through the group stages to reach the World Cup finals eight times has been bettered only by Italy and has been matched only by Brazil and Germany. Scotland are also special in that, in all the tournaments for which they have qualified, they have never gone into any World Cup match without there having been something at stake. This has resulted in a series of matches that have extracted every emotion from the Scottish fans. Scotland have never been boring.

The very best Scottish performances, both in qualifying and at the finals themselves, have all been of the fiery nature that is best associated with the Scots. For Scottish fans, those games have been as memorable as the very best that the Dutch, the Brazilians, the French and the other great sides in World Cup history have offered neutral Scottish observers. When the Scots are playing with skill and at speed, when it all clicks into place, it is an inspiring sight, unique in its style. As Ernst Happel, Holland's manager in 1978, said before their game with Scotland: 'My main worry over Scotland is their strength. I do not believe that the football is better technically than Dutch football. Often it is still kick and rush. But the players are strong and they seem to run forever.'

The Scots have always made a lot of friends during their World Cup exploits, on and off the field. Players such as Bobby Collins, Gordon Strachan, Archie Gemmill, Billy Bremner and Joe Jordan have embodied the Scottish blend of skill and spirit. At World Cup finals, neutral locals would often be uninterested when Scotland's games started but would soon be on the Scots' side, roused by the infectious passions of such players. The team is also blessed with supporters who are uncannily well-behaved. Their colourful, raucous, genuinely good-natured support has endeared them to people around the globe. They project a positive image of the Scots that a thousand tourist advertisements could not convey.

It was in the 1920s that Rimet, the president of FIFA, world football's organizing body, began kicking around the idea of a World Cup. Scotland had first joined FIFA in 1910, then left, along with England, in 1920. The Scots and the English rejoined in 1924 then, after further disagreements over administrative matters, left together again in 1928, two years before the first World Cup. The Scots would not rejoin until 1946, by which time FIFA's first three World Cups – in 1930, 1934 and 1938 – had taken place.

Qualification for the 1950 World Cup was open to the top two in that year's Home International Championship. Scotland finished second to England but the Scottish Football Association had decided that they would only participate in the finals if they were the British champions. Despite pleas from the English FA and players for the Scots to accompany them to the finals in Brazil, the SFA stubbornly refused to budge from their decision.

The 1960s brought even more crushing disappointment. During that decade, Scotland were blessed with a greater number of talented individuals than ever before – players such as Jimmy Johnstone, Bobby Murdoch, Pat Crerand, Denis Law, Jim Baxter, Tommy Gemmell – yet failed three times to qualify for the World Cup finals. In 1961, they were leading Czechoslovakia 2-1 in a play-off for a place in the finals. With seven minutes to go, the Czechs equalized and won 4-2 in extra-time. They would finish as runners-up to Brazil in the 1962 finals.

In 1965, several English club managers refused to allow their Scottish internationals to travel to Naples for a vital qualifier with Italy. A Scottish team that had been severely weakened by the absence of those players lost the game – 3-0 – and the chance of taking the World Cup from under the noses of Alf Ramsey's England in 1966. In 1969, a West German side including Franz Beckenbauer and Gerd Muller, among several distinguished others, finished above the Scots in their qualifying group and progressed to the semi-finals in Mexico in 1970.

By 1974, when Scotland were back in the frame, it was being lamented before the finals that they lacked class, that they just did not have the right quality of players they had had in the past. As so often, the Scots proved their critics' predictions wrong. That gift for producing the unexpected has helped make Scotland a team who contribute some of the most memorable moments to the World Cup party.

Ally McCoist, Kevin Gallacher, Tosh McKinlay and Colin Hendry celebrate after the 2-0 home victory over Latvia in October 1997 that saw Scotland clinch their place in the 1998 World Cup Finals.

THE UNLUCKY THIREEN

SWITZERLAND, 1954

'Our boys are rarin' to go. They have found a fine old confidence in themselves and, take it from me, they are not in the least worried about the much-ballyhooed opposition.' Tom Reid, Chairman of the SFA's International Committee in 1954

Andy Beattie outside the SFA's 1950s headquarters at Carlton Place in central Glasgow, which overlooked the River Clyde. Beattie was a part-time manager of Scotland, simultaneously carrying out his managerial duties at Huddersfield Town.

The first-ever international match took place in 1872 between Scotland and England in Glasgow. As the 1954 World Cup approached, it seemed appropriate that the same fixture was likely to decide whether Scotland would move into this newer sphere of international competition for the first time. This game would also be in Glasgow, on 3 April 1954 – just two months before the World Cup finals.

The England game was Scotland's final fixture of that season's Home International Championship. They had already obtained a home draw with Wales and a victory over Northern Ireland in Belfast. The possibility of qualifying for the World Cup in Switzerland – the prize for the 1953-54 season's Home International champions and runners-up – looked a strong one. The Scottish Football Association thus decided, for the first time ever, to appoint an individual to manage the national team.

It was very much a low-profile appointment, one that was accompanied by little fuss in Scotland. The man selected by the SFA International Committee was Andy Beattie, manager of Huddersfield Town. Celtic trainer Alec Dowdells was to be his assistant. Beattie had been a full-back for Scotland, winning the first of seven caps in 1937. Born in Aberdeenshire, he had, at 21, moved to Preston North End from junior side Inverurie Loco Works. In 1952 he became manager of Huddersfield, then in the Second Division. In his first season at the club they obtained promotion.

Beattie was appointed on 1 February 1954. He told 'Waverley' of the *Daily Record* from his Huddersfield home: 'I am thrilled and looking forward with pleasure to the day I take over. I cannot, in the meantime, make any comment about my duties, as I don't know yet what they will be. But you can rest assured that, whatever the task ahead of me, I'll approach it conscientiously. I consider I have been highly honoured and I will give all I have. The pleasure the news gives me is added to by the fact that I did not put myself forward for the job.'

On 5 February, Beattie travelled to Glasgow for a meeting with the SFA, where he was instructed as to his duties. His actual title was 'official in charge', not 'manager' or 'coach'. The task of picking the team remained with the SFA International Committee. It would then be presented to Beattie as a *fait accompli*. As 'official in charge' he would handle training and brief the players.

At that time, leading international football nations, such as Hungary and Uruguay, ploughed enormous resources into their national sides. They kept the players together for lengthy periods, playing and training. The strictures of Scottish and English club football made this impossible for the Scotland team, although the SFA did have the right to insist on having players' services for internationals. It was, however, proposed at a meeting of the SFA Council in February that Beattie should have the players for intensive training, preparation and friendlies from 3 May onwards should Scotland qualify for the World Cup.

With international football growing in importance in the post-war years, some clubs were beginning to worry about the demands the extra fixtures were placing on their players. Bailie John F. Wilson, chairman of Rangers, said: 'The taking away of a number of players from their clubs for many weeks carries serious implications.' Rangers were planning a close-season tour of Canada that would clash with the World Cup.

> *'You can rest assured that, whatever the task ahead of me, I'll approach it conscientiously. I consider I have been highly honoured and I will give all I have'*

Wilson addressed the SFA Council: 'When the SFA were originally given power to enforce clubs to release players for international matches, such a tournament as the World Cup wasn't contemplated. There was only in mind our three games with England, Ireland and Wales, and I question very much if it is legal to do what is now proposed. Rangers have always been loyal to the Association, have always been delighted to supply players for Scotland's teams, but in this instance my club are being asked to make a very big sacrifice.'

Rangers director George Brown told the SFA Council: 'This minute [to take players away for World Cup preparation] has serious implications. To what sort of coaching are the players to be subjected? Is it to be based on Rangers' tactics or Celtic's tactics? Are we to have our players' style of play altered? What is to be the effect on them of this process of indoctrination? The basis of national football in Scotland is club football. It is folly to imitate the continentals and produce eleven robots. Hungary is not the world's leading football country, as some people would have us believe. The leading football country is Britain because the game here is built on club football.'

By contrast, in Austria, the success of the national team took precedence over club football. Walter Rausch, Austria's coach since 1949, had established a playing style that all Austrian club sides had to follow. So if a player in the national team was replaced, the new man fitted seamlessly into the national side's pattern of play. Such a system would have been impossible for Scotland to adopt.

A fortnight before the England match, Scotland were dealt a double blow. Hibs' centre-forward Lawrie Reilly, the most accomplished centre-forward in Britain at the time, was to be confined to bed for two weeks with pleurisy. George Young, Rangers' right-back and Scotland's inspirational captain, was also declared unfit for the England match, because of a muscle strain.

The SFA's nine-man selection committee, chaired by Tom Reid of Partick Thistle, announced the following team for the England match ten days before the game: Farm, Haughney, Cox, Evans, Woodburn, Aitken, McKenzie, Johnstone, Henderson, Brown, Ormond. The team would play in the traditional 2-3-5 formation of the time. Mike Haughney, on his international debut, and Sammy Cox were the full-backs. Bobby Evans, Willie Woodburn and George Aitken looked a solid half-back line. They would be the fulcrum of a Scotland team that, overall, was pragmatic rather than exciting. Willie Ormond, however, the exciting Hibs left-winger, winning his first cap, looked an interesting choice. Ormond, a tenacious as well as skilful ball-player, had twice broken his leg.

The England team, captained by Billy Wright, featured Tom Finney, England's Footballer of the Year, at outside-right. Right-back Ron Staniforth was one of Beattie's players at Huddersfield.

The BBC asked the SFA if it could broadcast the Scotland v England game but was turned down, although it was given the option to broadcast highlights. The football authorities were worried about the effect TV would have on football. A joint announcement was made by the BBC and SFA that highlights of the match would be shown on Newsreel, two days after the game. Television, which would play such a significant role in transmitting the excitement of the World Cup, was just beginning to make inroads into British society. An Ekcovision receiver with a 15" screen was on sale for 76 guineas. Those watching their 15 minutes of highlights could use its 'spot-the-wobble' picture and sound control to get the best possible reception.

On the Wednesday before the England game, the Scottish party travelled to Largs on the Ayrshire coast. A doubt had arisen over the fitness of Rangers' talented centre-back Woodburn. He was troubled by a persistent knee ligament injury. When it was confirmed that Woodburn was unfit, Newcastle released their centre-half Frank Brennan. He joined the Scottish party at the Marine Hotel.

That evening, 31 March, the Scots learned that they had qualified for the World Cup finals for the first time. Wales had beaten Northern Ireland 2-1 in Wrexham,

Alec Dowdells (left), the Scotland trainer, defenders Sammy Cox (second left) and Frank Brennan (second right) and manager Andy Beattie relax at Largs before the match with England in April 1954.

guaranteeing Scotland second place in the Home International Championship. It was still important for Scotland to beat England, though. In January, FIFA had announced that the winners of the Home International Championship would be in a group with Belgium, Italy and Switzerland. The runners-up would be in with Austria, Uruguay and Czechoslovakia. Austria and Uruguay, the holders, were two of the favourites for the World Cup.

Scotland, needing the win, launched into frenzied attack from the start. After seven minutes, John McKenzie's corner reached Allan Brown, whose shot smacked off Staniforth's legs and into the English net. The unwilling assistance from his own Huddersfield player seemed to indicate that the luck was going Beattie's way. But that was where his luck would end that afternoon. Seven minutes on, Finney floated away from Cox and set up Broadis for England's equalizer. Six minutes after half-time, Finney again sidestepped Cox, this time crossing for Nicholls to head England into the lead. Midway through the half, another header, this time from Allen, made it 3-1 to England. Seven minutes from time, Finney dodged round Cox yet again and presented Mullen with the third English headed goal of the match.

A minute from time, Ormond's lob made the final score 4-2 to England. It did little to still the Scots lament that arose from the terraces in response to their team's poverty of performance. Only wingers McKenzie and Ormond received any credit from the afternoon's exertions. The rest could consider their positions in the team under serious threat.

A week later, on Sunday 11 April, Austria took on Hungary in Vienna. In 1950, Austria had become the first foreign side to beat Scotland at Hampden. Five members of that team also took the field for the match with Hungary, seen as world champions-elect. Andy Beattie was in Vienna to see Austria lose unluckily when a shot from Kocsis was deflected into goal by Happel. Austria were dominant throughout and twice had shots cleared off the line.

Meanwhile, news came in mid-April that Lawrie Reilly, one of the few Scots with the technical ability to match that of the Austrians, had been admitted to an Edinburgh hospital for intensive treatment. He did hope to be on the continent in the summer – for a recuperative holiday.

On 17 April, selector Jimmy Beattie went south with Tom Reid to watch Tommy Docherty and Willie Cunningham perform well for Preston North End against Chelsea. Neil Mochan, one of the inspired individuals behind Celtic's first championship for 16 years, was also in the frame for World Cup selection. Cunningham and Mochan were

Frank Brennan intervenes in an England attack during the 1954 international at Hampden. Willie Ormond (left) and Bobby Evans (centre) are the Scotland players looking on.

uncapped; Docherty had acquired three caps over the previous two years.

Scotland's matches would be in Basle and Zurich. Scotland had an option on tickets for a third of the capacity at each stadium. In the 1950s, however, only the wealthy could afford any sort of holiday abroad, and few supporters were expected to follow Scotland to Switzerland. The St Jakob Stadium in Basle was being built at a cost of £25,000. It would have a capacity of 49,000 and its most distinguished feature would be an ultra-modern cantilevered stand. Ticket prices for the first round of the World Cup ranged from six shillings and eight pence to one pound, six shillings and eight pence. At the time, price of entry to a Scottish First Division match was around four shillings.

When the 18-man preliminary squad was chosen on 21 April, no Rangers players were included. Young, Woodburn and Cox, instead, would go on Rangers' tour of Canada. Both Norway and Finland were expected to be undemanding opposition in a trio of pre-World Cup friendlies arranged for May. The Norwegians had initially been taught football by Scots coaches, but by the 1950s they had turned to Austrian coaches for their football education. In the 34th minute of their match at Hampden, Scotland scored the only goal of the game. Norway's goalkeeper Hansen should have held on to inside-right George Hamilton's header but he lost it and it leaked over the line.

> *'The appointment of a team manager was the best thing we have done for long enough. It's working perfectly.'*

Hampden did not yet have floodlights so the game had kicked off in the afternoon. Many workers in the 25,000 crowd had given up a shift to go to the game. Midway through the second half, disgusted by the Scots' poor performance, the fans switched allegiance to the Norwegian part-timers. They gave the Scottish players a slow handclap in the closing minutes and as they left the pitch.

The selectors had now used 27 players in four internationals during the 1953–54 season. After the Norway game further changes looked likely. This was hardly conducive to producing a settled side with the type of intricate knowledge of each other's play essential to top-class international football. The three selectors entrusted with selection for the World Cup were Tom Reid of Partick Thistle, the chairman of the international committee, George Carroll of Airdrieonians and Andrew Beattie of Albion Rovers. 'The appointment of a team manager was the best thing we have done for long enough. It's working perfectly,' said Reid before Scotland faced Norway in Oslo. The 1-1 draw yielded an improved performance. Scotland's goal, in the 11th minute, was scored by McKenzie. Scotland played some impressive football although they were again lacking incision up front. In the 2-1 win in Finland on 25 May, Ormond and Johnstone were the scorers. Again, Scotland enjoyed good build-up play but were feeble in attack.

Herr Hahn, the Norwegian team manager, a former Austrian international, said of his native country: 'We don't seem to have the right type of forward at the moment and it won't need a defence of extraordinary skill or strength to outwit them and keep them from the net.' He suggested that Austria were not as good as they had been when beating Scotland 4-0 in 1951, a match dubbed 'The Battle of Vienna'.

At the end of May, following the Scottish League's AGM, the three selectors Reid, Beattie and Carroll, taking into account written and verbal reports on the tour from Andy Beattie, chose their World Cup 13. Each country could submit a list of 22 players to FIFA, and it was still not too late for Scotland to take a squad of 22 to Switzerland. Yet at such a crucial stage, the SFA Council could not reconvene – it had had its final meeting of the season. It was apparently impossible for the SFA to hold a special meeting for the World Cup despite growing concern – even among some of its members – that Scotland's squad was far too small. It contained, for example, just one goalkeeper – Fred Martin of Aberdeen.

Still, with him to Switzerland Beattie would take his lucky acorn, gathered from the floor of Sherwood Forest before a Huddersfield match at Nottingham Forest. 'Each of our party, on learning that an acorn from the tree was considered a lucky

Bobby Johnstone was one of Scotland's few successes against England in 1954. Johnstone, who was versatile enough to play in any attacking position, won 17 caps and also played for Great Britain against the Rest of Europe.

charm, helped himself to one. Since then I actually have experienced some good fortune in football. For instance, Huddersfield that season secured promotion.'

On 30 May Austria defeated Norway 5-0 in Vienna. Herr Hahn, in Vienna with Norway, said: 'Scotland are quite a speedy moving team, but that is not enough. Much more will be needed if the Scots hope to win over the brilliant technique and accurate passing of the well-knit Austrians.' The Norwegian players themselves offered the opinion that they had played as well as in the games against Scotland but that at no time had they given the Austrians the problems they had given the Scots. A week later, Austria, with a sumptuous display of teamwork and technical brilliance, defeated Milan 7-0. In Vienna, bookmakers had Scotland at 10-1 to beat Austria and there was amazement that Scotland were taking just 13 players to Switzerland. The Austrians were, of course, taking their full complement of 22.

In pre-World Cup training at Somerset Park, Ayr, the 13 were assisted by 10 Partick Thistle and Celtic players, who made up the numbers for 11-a-side games. Among them was Jock Stein, then a centre-back at Celtic.

On 12 June Scotland's World Cup hopes took wing on the 9 a.m. flight from Prestwick to Switzerland. As FIFA put the final touches to the World Cup ground rules in Switzerland, Scotland and England thwarted a move to allow substitutes in the World Cup. The Brits directly opposed the proposal and threatened to walk out of the World Cup if it was adopted.

Matches in the 1954 World Cup were not staggered for the benefit of TV. On 16 June, four games started at 6 p.m. British time: Uruguay v Czechoslovakia; Brazil v Mexico; France v Yugoslavia; and Scotland v Austria. Scottish viewers could tune in at 5.55 p.m. to the only available channel – the BBC – to watch … France v Yugoslavia. Nor was there full radio coverage of the Scotland match – only the occasional bulletin during the evening.

Tom Reid was moved to say, shortly before the match with Austria: 'Our boys are rarin' to go. They have found a fine old confidence in themselves and, take it from me, they are not in the least worried about the much-ballyhooed opposition. I believe we shall win – a belief that has been greatly strengthened since coming out here. Our forwards have been instructed to go all out for an early goal, knowing from experience that the continentals don't like to have to fight back. Special emphasis has been laid on the necessity of hard, but always fair, tackling. This should knock some of the funny notions out of the heads of the Austrians.'

WILLIE WOODBURN

Conditions were good for Scotland. There had been several showers in the days before the game and the evening was cool. There were 25,000 fans in the stadium, including a smattering of Scots supporters. Scotland, as Reid had promised, went into the game determined to act rather than react. In the early stages they made sure they got to the ball first. They also produced an essence of constructive football that could not have been anticipated from the evidence of their previous matches. The wholesome Neil 'Smiler' Mochan led the line with verve and vigour. Early on, two Mochan crosses had Austrian goalkeeper Schmied flapping as he attempted to deal with them. At the back, Doug Cowie, Jimmy Davidson and Docherty maintained close concentration in breaking up the studied Austrian attacks. They were well supplemented by full-backs Cunningham and John Aird.

One particular run from Mochan, started from the middle of the field, had the Austrians on their heels. On reaching the edge of the penalty area he was knocked over by left-back Ernst Happel. The Scots claimed a penalty; Belgian referee Laurent Franken gave an indirect free-kick. The Austrians cleared the resultant Scots effort but within minutes Mochan just failed to reach a cross from McKenzie. The faintest touch would have put Scotland ahead.

With 35 minutes gone, Austrian inside-left Probst knocked the ball to his winger, Koerner. Koerner took the ball forwards then spun it across the Scots' goalmouth. Probst, still running, moved into space close to the corner of the six-yard box. From there he squeezed the ball past the advancing Fred Martin. Aird, close to the goal-line, missed connecting with the goalbound shot by inches as he stretched for it, off-balance, with his right foot. It was 1-0 to Austria.

In the early part of the second half, Scotland struggled to maintain their momentum. Their passing started to falter. They also found it difficult to deal with the Austrians' famous gamesmanship, now more in evidence. Weak refereeing from Franken was in evidence as the Austrian elbows and boots cracked against their opponents' bones. The Scots eventually revived. A lobbed header from Ormond looped just over the bar. With 10 minutes remaining, Mochan moved to the right wing, with McKenzie taking his place at centre-forward. It was Mochan, however, who, in the final minute, got a shot on target. His strike eluded several Austrian defenders and Schmied watched the ball sail goalwards. At the last, the goalkeeper stretched, and, at the second attempt, stopped the ball entering his net.

'I am delighted that the boys are now serving up good football. It is up to them to finish off that grand approach work. The spirit of the whole eleven tonight was something to be proud of,' said Andy Beattie. At home, the 1-0 defeat was greeted as a minor victory.

The Scots nation eagerly awaited the next game. Uruguay had laboured to a 2-0 win over the Czechs with a goal in each half from Miguez and Schiaffino. At that World Cup, FIFA had ruled that, in the group stages, each team would only play twice: Scotland would not meet the Czechs, only Uruguay and Austria. If Austria beat the Czechs and Scotland beat Uruguay, Scotland would play Uruguay again for a place in the next round. The same Scotland team was announced for the match with Uruguay on 19 June. Cunningham had needed an X-ray for a shoulder knock but was passed fit.

The performance against Austria had been one of Scotland's most impressive since the war. On the evening before the Uruguay match, however, the Scottish team was dealt a morale-busting blow. Andy Beattie announced he was quitting as Scotland's 'official in charge'. He denied reports that he would leave immediately after the Uruguay game, win, lose or draw. He said he would continue as long as Scotland remained in the World Cup but admitted there had been internal disagreements with SFA officials in the past. His lack of control over team selection had been an insurmountable problem.

The match with Uruguay was live on TV and, regardless of Beattie's decision, Scots crowded round their televisions in anticipation. There were 43,000 at the match, the biggest crowd up to that point for a match in the Swiss World Cup. Eight Scottish army pipers performed for the crowd beforehand. This time the game was played in a smothering heat. The conditions looked more likely to suit the Uruguayans than the Scots. Uruguay had won the World Cup in 1950 through a fine percolation of South American natural talent, positional discipline and exceptional fitness.

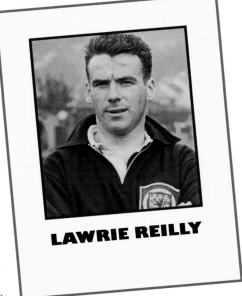

LAWRIE REILLY

As the match began, the Swiss fans, impressed by Scotland's showing against Austria, approximated a Hampden roar by getting firmly behind the Scots. Suitably inspired, Scotland made a stirring start. In the fourth minute, Brown then Mochan miskicked in front of goal with only Uruguayan goalkeeper Maspoli to beat.

After 17 minutes a Fernie pass ended up with Uruguayan outside-right Abadie. He swept away from Aird and crossed for Borges to open the scoring. By then, Scotland were being made to look backwards by the Uruguayans; oppressed by the Uruguayans' covering and positional sense, the Scots were constantly forced to pass to teammates to their rear. On the half-hour, it was Docherty's turn to give away possession. Miguez' scoring short provided severe punishment.

The Uruguayans did not relax. Cruz picked up the ball just inside his own half. The Scots seemed paralysed into inaction as they attempted to deal with his advance and could only retreat in the face of his pace. He closed in on the target and let fly a shot that Martin did well to save. Shortly before half-time, Mochan's pass put Brown in a good position with only the grounded goalkeeper between him and the net. The inside-left hesitated and the chance was gone. It remained 2-0 to Uruguay at the interval, during which a lone piper on the terraces entertained the crowd.

Three minutes after the restart, a Docherty pass was intercepted by outside-left Borges. The winger's acceleration saw him bypass right-back Cunningham without a second glance before curling the ball round Martin for his second and Uruguay's third goal.

At that point, it appeared that several Scottish players, depressed by the hopeless task ahead of them and drained by the severity of the heat, gave up the cause as a lost one. The Scots were also thoroughly disoriented by Martinez, nominally a left-back, who had a free role behind the forward line, a tactic that British sides found great difficulty in combating. In training at Ayr, Beattie had practised stopping a mobile, continually moving centre-forward; Martinez created an equally difficult extra problem.

After his goal, Borges was carried shoulder-high back to his own half by his teammates. His colleague on the opposite wing, Abadie, gathered some glory for himself in the 55th minute by flicking the ball past Martin from a narrow angle. On the hour, Borges again slithered through the Scottish defence to make it 5-0 with a shot that he placed carefully between Martin and his post.

Brown and McKenzie had half-chances to get one back for Scotland but their efforts were dealt with comfortably by Maspoli. The goalkeeper was put under more severe pressure by a Mochan effort 15 minutes from time. The fierceness of his shot saw it roll from the goalkeeper's grasp but he managed to clutch it before it crossed his

Lawrie Reilly missed the 1954 World Cup through illness. He won further caps for Scotland after the Swiss World Cup and when the next World Cup came around, in 1958, he was still only 29. That year, however, he was forced to retire from football through injury. His presence at either tournament would have been of immeasurable value to Scotland.

line. With seven minutes remaining, Miguez made it 6-0; two minutes on, Abadie finished the scoring at 7-0. By the end, the Swiss were jeering the Scots' every move. The lone piper played on. The Uruguayans had body-checked, handled frequently, kicked and gouged throughout. Referee Orlandini of Italy had, however, controlled the game fairly, cautioning three Uruguayans and two Scots.

'I do not want to use the weather as an excuse,' said Beattie afterwards. 'But I think everybody admits it was pretty hot. The Uruguayans are a very fine side and their victory was fully deserved. I do think, however, that the two first-half goals might sadly not have happened had we been luckier in the opening stages. The game might have developed differently.'

'I could hardly breathe after the first 20 minutes,' said Ormond. 'They were not so fast themselves but they took every opportunity to use the ball and make it do the work,' said Davidson.

Troccoli, Uruguay's team manager, said: 'The result is very satisfactory, of course, but the team's performance was not perfect, especially during the first half, when they should have shown more determination and fighting spirit. The team has not yet reached the form which is needed to win the World Cup. We consider the game against Scotland as another stage in the build-up of our team for the decisive game – the final of the World Cup. The Scottish team was too weak to give the result much relevance. I expect that the weather, which was even a bit hot for us, was the main cause of the Scottish collapse.'

Juan Lopez, Uruguay's coach, afterwards paid tribute to Alec Raeside, a Scot who was famous in Uruguay for his input to the game while Uruguayan coach. 'It was Alec who taught us the basic principles of the game,' said Lopez.

Scots had done much to teach others the game of football in its earliest years. It was now up to Scotland to educate themselves in the new ways of the world and its cup before the next tournament came around in Sweden in 1958.

THE SCOTS FLOWER

SWEDEN, 1958

'I aim not to have a team content merely to put up a respectable show in Sweden, but one that will take the field with the aim of winning the global trophy.'

Matt Busby on becoming Scotland's team manager

Scotland goalkeeper Tommy Younger and centre-half George Young ensure that Alfredo Di Stefano is kept a safe distance from the ball during the stirring 1957 World Cup qualifier against Spain at Hampden.

In recognition of their role in the game's development, FIFA had allowed Scotland the cosy familiarity of the Home International Championship as the means of qualifying for the 1954 World Cup. For the 1958 World Cup, there were no such favours. Scotland were placed in a tough European qualifying section. They would face Spain and Switzerland in a three-team group with only one country qualifying for the finals. The Spanish were widely regarded as favourites not just to win the group but to win the 1958 World Cup. The Swiss, the hosts of the previous World Cup, were looking to build on their quarter-final placing in that tournament. The physical and psychological problems faced in these home and away fixtures would make for another steep and rugged incline on Scotland's international learning curve.

The first qualifier would be against Spain at Hampden on 8 May 1957. Despite Spain's status, tickets for the match sold slowly. Stand seats were expensive at 30 shillings and 21 shillings; but a place on the terracing cost a reasonable three shillings and sixpence. Four days beforehand, 80 percent of tickets had not been sold. So the SFA decided the game could not be shown on television and that instead of the game being all-ticket, cash would be taken at the turnstiles.

In addition to increased competition between national sides, international club competitions were now under way. In 1955, the European Cup – the first Europe-wide club competition – had begun. Real Madrid had won the first trophy and had just claimed their place in their second European Cup final. Five of those Real players were in the Spanish squad for the match with Scotland. They were led by the inspirational Alfredo Di Stefano, now 33, Argentinian-born but a naturalized Spaniard.

> *Di Stefano denied that the Spaniards were bad travellers: 'We play good football anywhere.'*

Relaxedly drawing on a cigarette on arrival at Glasgow's Abbotsinch airport, Di Stefano denied that the Spaniards were bad travellers: 'We play good football anywhere.' Mateos, his inside-right, casually blew smoke rings beside him.

George Young, Scotland's captain, said: 'If we are to believe all reports, we are asked to meet a team of supermen. The Spaniards are described to us as the greatest team in the world, and we are expected, no doubt, to go to Hampden feeling very much inferior. Take it from me, we will face the opposition with this thought: they are just eleven men in jerseys. We are as good as, if not better, than them.'

The Spaniards themselves reckoned they were the best team in Europe, if not the world. In the Scotland team that lined up against them, only Tommy Docherty, now at left-half, was a survivor from the 1954 World Cup finals. The side, announced a fortnight before the match, was: Younger, Caldow, Hewie, McColl, Young, Docherty, Smith, Collins, Mudie, Baird, Ring.

The match kicked off at 6 p.m.; Hampden still did not have floodlights. On the evening, 89,000 turned up. Those expecting sweet skills from the Spanish were disappointed. Wild tackling and an emphasis on the physical suggested that they had come prepared for a battle. Once in action, they discovered the Scots concentrating on a cohesive passing game. Thus the expected roles were reversed and the Scots proved better at adapting to the Spaniards' usual style than the Spaniards were at their idea of a tough-tackling British game.

After 24 minutes Jackie Mudie put Scotland ahead. His shot came off the bar and he got to the rebound first to head it into the net. Five minutes later, Kubala miskicked in front of the Scottish goal; in doing so, he sent Tommy Younger the wrong way for a lucky equalizer. Four minutes from half-time, Olivella took out Tommy Ring inside the Spanish penalty area. German referee Albert Busch awarded a penalty. Hewie's kick was half-stopped by goalkeeper Ramallets but the ball still slipped into the net.

In the 50th minute Di Stefano found space on the edge of the Scottish penalty area. Younger blocked his shot but it fell neatly for Luis Suarez to equalize. Late in the half the Scots went ahead again. Collins passed to Mudie and his shot dipped over Ramallets. Ten minutes from time, Collins again supplied Mudie for a scoring shot that made it 4-2 and left the Spaniards with no way back. It had been a rainy night and the Spaniards hadn't enjoyed playing on the soft Hampden surface. There was too much 'give' in it for their usual game.

The away match with Switzerland took place 11 days later. The second half was televised 'live' in Britain. The Scotland team was unchanged from the one that had beaten Spain at Hampden. Scotland wore orange pants borrowed from the Swiss because of a new FIFA ruling that opposing teams had to wear different-coloured shorts. Scotland lost an early goal, but a well-taken header from Bobby Collins put them level. Then, 11 minutes from time, another precise header, this time from Mudie, gave them a 2-1 victory but it was a wan performance in comparison to the one against Spain.

The Scots moved on to Stuttgart for a friendly with the world champions, West Germany. A crowd of 77,000 watched as Collins, a ball of fire at inside-right, gave Scotland the lead after 20 minutes. Mudie made it 2-0 on 33 minutes, then Collins, with his second long-range shot of the day, put Scotland 3-0 up on 54. The Germans got one back to make the final score 3-1. The Scottish national team's rehabilitation after 1954 seemed close to completion.

On reaching Madrid for the return with Spain, the Scots were able to examine, at their leisure, the Spanish line-up. The Scots, however, announced they would keep their selection quiet until the day of the match. Spanish technical officials had watched Scotland's recent matches. It was feared that an early announcement of the team would give the Spaniards too much time to plan counter-measures against players they knew well. When the team was announced, Hearts' Dave Mackay was at right-half. That was the minor surprise. The major one was the omission of George Young. Bobby Evans, centre-half against West Germany, retained his place.

The deception over the team lines did not work. This time, the Spaniards relied on their natural skills. Gento, their winger, and Di Stefano orchestrated a blanket domination of the game. Spain won 4-1.

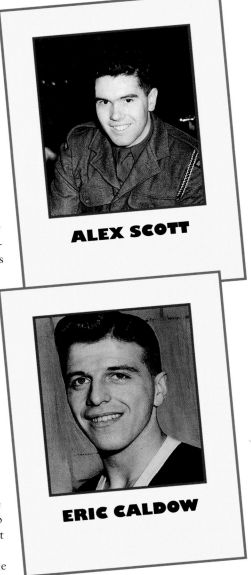

ALEX SCOTT

ERIC CALDOW

Young had requested that he be rested for the West Germany game as he was carrying an injury. He had also announced his intention to quit international football after the Madrid match. It was rumoured that this, together with his decision to miss the German game, may have been held against him by SFA officials.

Di Stefano said after the match in Madrid: 'At Hampden we lost team balance when Scotland took the lead at 3-2. One of the reasons we failed was because I could not tempt Young out of position. I used all my ingenuity but there he was, always looming up as a barrier, impossible to pass.' Don Manuel Vallina, sole selector of the Spanish team, said: 'Scotland's defence was not nearly compact enough. Actually, to my mind, it had no plan. It offered our forwards opportunities they should never have been given. Although at Hampden I thought Young was on the slow side, I did recognize that he could organize a defensive system that was very difficult to get through.'

Scotland, however, remained on course to qualify from the group. A draw at home to Switzerland had left the Spaniards a point behind the Scots in the qualifying table. If Scotland defeated the Swiss at Hampden in November, they would go to the World Cup finals. A draw would almost certainly lead to a play-off with Spain at a neutral venue.

The Swiss game started at 2.30 p.m. to catch the last of the November daylight. A crowd of 56,811 saw Archie Robertson open the scoring for Scotland. Then a mishit Tommy Docherty pass was intercepted by Riva for the equalizer. Mudie put Scotland ahead again. But it was a precarious advantage; this was a highly determined Swiss side. That was emphasized when Alex Parker cleared a Chiesa shot off the line midway through the second half. The next minute, Alex Scott, looking several yards offside, took hold of a pass from Collins. Scott glanced back to check if the referee had blown for offside but was allowed to proceed. Scott's resultant goal put Scotland 3-1 up. The referee was surrounded by protesting Swiss. In the final 20 minutes, Younger's saves rescued Scotland time and time again as the Swiss angrily hit back. Ten minutes from the end, Vonlanden's close-range shot hit the roof of the Scottish net to make it 3-2.

Tommy Younger, who had been impressive throughout the qualifiers, said: 'It was

Matt Busby (below right) with former Scottish international Willie Thornton. Busby was tragically prevented from managing Scotland at the 1958 World Cup but the following season he took charge of the team for the Home Internationals before deciding to concentrate on his job at Manchester United. In 1959, Andy Beattie took over from Busby for Beattie's second spell as Scotland manager.

a marvellous victory for Scotland. It must be understood that the boys were under a strain which affected their play, because we had to win to qualify.'

On 9 January 1958, the SFA announced that, this being a World Cup year, Scotland was to have an international team manager. The following week, the day after his Manchester United side had defeated Red Star Belgrade 2-1 in the European Cup quarter-final, Matt Busby was named as Scotland's team manager for the World Cup finals in Sweden. 'I am delighted to accept the invitation. It is a great honour,' said Busby. 'I can only do my best. I hope I can do something to help Scotland win the World Cup. I aim not to have a team content merely to put up a respectable show in Sweden, but one that will take the field with the aim of winning the global trophy.'

Unlike Andy Beattie, Busby would sit with the panel of selectors as they discussed the make-up of the Scotland team. He was to have input into those discussions. Strong character that he was, Busby would ensure that his input was acted upon.

On Monday 3 February, outside-left Stewart Imlach of Nottingham Forest was the 'find' in an SFA trial match between Scotland and the Scottish League. There were 45,000 at Easter Road to see the Scotland Select's 3-2 victory but Matt Busby was not among them. He was in Belgrade with Manchester United for the second leg of their European Cup quarter-final. On 5 February, they reached the semi-finals with a 3-3 draw. On the flight back, the party made a stopover at Munich. As their plane attempted to take off it crashed. Twenty-one people died immediately, including seven United players. Matt Busby, severely injured, went into a coma and was placed in intensive care at Munich's Rechts der Isar hospital. He received regular blood transfusions and was placed in an oxygen tent. Surgeons put his chances of survival at only 50-50. He would make a recovery but it would be a slow and painful one.

Representatives of the other competing World Cup nations expressed their sadness at Busby's absence at the World Cup draw, which was made live on TV in Stockholm on Saturday 8 February. Scotland were drawn to play in Group Two against Yugoslavia in Vasteras on 8 June; Paraguay in Norrköping on 11 June; and France in

Orebro on 15 June. The new SFA Secretary, Willie Allan, cast his eye over the draw and pronounced: 'If, as I am confident we will be, we are successful in the initial matches in the grouping, I don't think the final itself is beyond us.'

The squad would be based at Turnberry, in Ayrshire, from 12–16 May and again on 19–23 May. For training, they would use Girvan Amateurs' ground. As in 1954, Scotland were fast approaching the World Cup finals without an established first eleven. There was some margin for error: this time a squad of 22 was going to the World Cup. In March the selectors watched Denis Law, a 17-year-old inside-forward with Huddersfield Town. He was named in the initial squad of 40 – lingering evidence of Busby's advice to the selectors. The SFA had no contingency plans to replace Busby, still recuperating, as team manager; they continued to hope he would be fit for the finals.

Tom Reid, chairman of the Scotland selectors, took charge for the Home International with England on 19 April. The team picked for the match emphasized Scotland's problems. The defensive element looked settled and reliable but the forward line was largely untried at international level. Jim Forrest, George Herd and Jimmy Murray were all winning their first caps. Outside-left Tommy Ewing of Partick Thistle was on his second cap. Centre-forward Jackie Mudie was the only forward with any real international experience. Scotland sagged to a demoralizing 4-0 defeat. The forward line, with the exception of Mudie, looked slow. The World Cup was less than two months away.

One possible antidote to Scotland's ills was lost days later when Denis Law had to withdraw from consideration. He would be out of action for six weeks with an ankle ligament injury.

A chance to disperse the gloom descending on Scottish World Cup matters came in early May when Hungary arrived in Glasgow. Six changes were made from the team that played England. Tommy Younger was Scotland's captain for this game. He sought Busby's advice on how Scotland should play the match beforehand and, on the evening, Younger was in excellent form in the Scotland goal.

'We are going to play football. The emphasis will be playing football in the old traditional Scottish way – at a faster pace.'

A 1-1 draw in swamp conditions saw Scotland match the Hungarians for skilful play. Suddenly, all was right with the world. 'We are back on the rails,' said Haig Gordon, an SFA international committee selector. The goal certainly deserved praise, Aberdeen outside-right Graham Leggat's cross being headed powerfully past the Hungarian goalkeeper by the mobile Mudie.

Dawson Walker, the squad's trainer, was in charge of team organization during World Cup preparation at Girvan Amateurs' ground. He held nightly conferences at which the players had the chance to put forward their views. 'When we go to Sweden we are not looking for the breaks,' he said. 'We are going to play football. The emphasis will be on playing football in the old traditional Scottish way – at a faster pace.'

In Warsaw, for the Scots' final friendly before travelling to Sweden, the same team that had drawn with Hungary faced the Poles. In front of 70,000, Scotland played a refined passing game. Collins, acting as a free man in the forward line, got both the goals in a 2-1 win. One Polish newspaper said the Scots had produced 'the best performance of technical skill seen in Warsaw since the war'.

On arrival in Sweden on 2 June it was confirmed that the same 11 as had played in the previous two games would confront Yugoslavia. 'We are producing goal-making play,' said Tommy Younger who, as well as being captain, gave the team talks in Busby's prolonged absence. 'There is nothing haphazard about it. The moves are being calculated and they are proving successful. I believe the lads up front will oblige us with punch at close quarters.

A new development taken up by the Scots for this World Cup was to play practice games at the same time as kick-off. On 5 June they enjoyed a 2-0 win over amateur side Eskilstuna, the town in which the Scottish squad was based for the World Cup group games. Collins and Mudie were the scorers.

The Swedes, in their egalitarian way, had decided to take their World Cup to as many venues as possible, large and small. Scotland's first game was on Sunday 8 June against Yugoslavia in the small town of Vasteras. There were just 9,500 to see the match, which began at 7 p.m. British time. After six minutes, Petakovic sped into the Scots' box and aimed a low shot at goal. Younger misjudged it, the ball flew past him and Yugoslavia were 1-0 ahead.

Scotland took that as their cue to dominate the game. Collins gave an ample demonstration of the effectiveness of his new role as he shuttled between the forwards and the middle of the field. The Slavs found it impossible to pin him down. Eventually, Sekularac, the Yugoslavian inside-left, smacked him on the mouth. Collins, always a tough competitor, responded with a flurry of punches. The Swiss referee remained neutral, ignoring the exchange. When he blew for half-time Scotland were still 1-0 down.

Three minutes after the break, the 35-year-old Turnbull, calm and collected at right-half, eked out a cross that Murray met with his head for the equalizer. Scotland were exerting a hypnotic degree of control on the match but despite their possession they failed to pour on the goals. Evans, at centre-half, was magnificent. However, a warning of the danger of failing to capitalize on this superiority was offered when Veselinovic hit the post.

With a quarter of an hour remaining, Imlach crossed, Yugoslavian goalkeeper Beara leaped for the ball and held it. But as he dropped back to earth he collided with Mudie and the ball rolled over the Yugoslavian line. Mudie was penalized and referee Wyssling disallowed the goal. The match ended 1-1. Mudie disingenuously said of his disallowed goal: 'I rose with Beara for the ball. He caught hold of the leather, but without my touching it he actually threw it over his left shoulder into the net. I honestly believe it was a goal and should have been allowed to stand as such.'

Imlach had picked up a knee injury in the Yugoslavia game. It was announced that his replacement at outside-left by Willie Fernie would be the only change for the Paraguay game in Norrköping the following Wednesday. Collins had left the field in

Tommy Younger, the Scotland goalkeeper, punches the ball clear during a Home International with Wales. George Young (number 5) provides him with cover. Unusually for a goalkeeper, Younger was made Scotland captain after Young retired from international football in 1957.

Vasteras with two loose teeth but he was fit for the Paraguayans. However, shortly before the match began, the Scots made two late changes. Alex Parker came in for John Hewie at full-back and Robertson replaced Murray in the forward line.

While Scotland were playing Yugoslavia, squad members Archie Robertson and Johnny Coyle had been in Norrköping watching France defeat Paraguay 7-3. Robertson reported that the Paraguayans were over-reliant on physical strength. France, he said, were a highly underrated, attractive, effective team.

On the BBC in Scotland, the match shown on 11 June was England v Brazil, which kicked off at the same time – 8 p.m. – as the Scots' game with Paraguay. This time Scotland were watched by 11,700 spectators. For the second successive game, Scotland got off to a poor start. After four minutes, Paraguay's inside-left Re switched the ball quickly to outside-left Aguero. He found space in front of the Scottish goal and nicked the ball through the outrushing Younger's legs for the opening goal. The goalkeeper looked badly at fault. Scotland came through further early pressure without suffering any more damage. They now eased into their patient, passing football and waited for the chance to get the equalizer. Midway through the half, Arevalo, Paraguay's right-back, cleared from in front of his goal with an overhead kick. It fell to Bobby Collins, 10 yards from goal. He had time to control the ball before shooting narrowly over the bar. After 22 minutes, Robertson took on Mudie's pass for an easier chance. With only goalkeeper Agulia to beat he sent the ball straight into the Paraguayan's arms.

Three minutes later, the Scots' subtlety paid off. Fernie made a penetrating run, then picked out Collins. He eased the ball on to Mudie. The centre-forward's pass was looked after carefully by Leggat who beat Agulia with his shot. Arevalo, however, raced back to clear the ball off the line. It span back to Mudie who volleyed it home to make it 1-1. With seconds to go in the half, Parodi sent a long pass in the direction of his outside-left Amarilla. Parker failed to intercept it, the winger zipped away from him and crossed. Re's shot hit Younger, then a post, then the Scottish net. Paraguay celebrated a 2-1 half-time lead.

Early in the second half, Mudie took a heavy blow from a Paraguayan defender.

Between 1955 and 1958, Tommy Younger won 24 Scotland caps but he would not pull on an international jersey again after Bill Brown replaced him for the match with France in the World Cup finals in Sweden.

Combining skill and competitiveness in equal measures, Bobby Collins was the hub of the action in all seven of Scotland's World Cup matches in 1957 and 1958. First capped in 1951 at the age of 20, he won his final cap in 1965, aged 34. Two lengthy periods when he was out of favour meant that he won a total of just 31 caps.

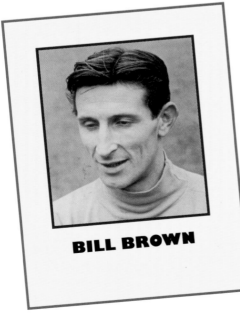

BILL BROWN

He spent several minutes off the park receiving treatment. While he was sidelined, Caldow headed a Paraguayan scoring effort off the line. As the half progressed, Scotland struggled more and more. Re should have made it 3-1 but from close range the inside left screwed his shot wide of the goal.

With 15 minutes remaining, a Paraguayan cross was intercepted by Younger. The ball slipped from his grasp and Romero poked it into the Scots net. The best goal of the match arrived a minute later. Collins, who had again been involved in some running battles, collected the ball in the final third of the field. He darted past a couple of defenders and shot high into the net from just outside the six-yard box. Inspired by that, Scotland pressed hard for the equalizer. In the final seconds, as the Scots swarmed around his goal, Aguila was left stretched out on the ground but neither Leggat nor Mudie could put the ball in the net from close range. The 3-2 defeat meant Scotland were now bottom of Group 2.

The Scotland players were being paid £50 a game. In their final group match, with France, several players would have the first chance to earn themselves some World Cup money and Scotland a place in the quarter-finals. Mudie had been injured when being kicked in the back while lying on the ground after a tackle – he had suffered extensive bruising. It would be a late decision whether he or Coyle should play at centre-forward. Leggat had ended up with a fractured wrist following a tussle with the Paraguayan goalkeeper. Hewie and Murray were still recovering from injuries sustained against the Yugoslavs. Evans had a groin strain. It meant that Scotland's team against France would not be named until close to kick-off.

When the team was announced the most notable change was not prompted by injury. Bill Brown made his debut in goal in place of Younger, who had been jittery throughout the Paraguay game. It was just one of six alterations to the team that had played Paraguay. Young Dave Mackay, whose hard-tackling style had made him a controversial figure in Scotland the previous season, stiffened the half-back line in place of Cowie, a precise ball-player who had watched the Paraguay game pass him by. Evans, now fit, took Younger's place as captain.

The French had lost 3-2 to Yugoslavia in their second group game. It had been a bad result for Scotland: now the French needed a win as badly as Scotland did. Back home that Sunday afternoon, at 2 p.m., via the Eurovision link and in association with FIFA, viewers of BBC and STV saw Sweden v Wales. At 6.40 p.m the following Tuesday, the BBC would show 20 minutes of highlights of Scotland v France.

The match took place in Orebro in front of 13,500 spectators. After two minutes, Scotland appeared to have lost their third consecutive early goal. Vincent, the French outside-right, steered a strong shot towards the target but Brown sprang at the ball to knock it over his bar. Sammy Baird went almost as close for Scotland.

In the 21st minute, Fontaine took possession of a Piantoni pass inside the Scottish half. Accelerating at a pace the Scots' backs couldn't cope with, he drove deep into the penalty area. His eventual cross was met by Kopa, the French inside-forward. A quick flick of his foot put the Scots a goal behind. Mackay responded positively, connecting with the ball several yards outside the French penalty area. His low, hard shot tested Abbes, the French goalkeeper. Baird followed up, looking for the rebound. When he was sent tumbling, Argentinian referee Juan Brazzi awarded a penalty. French players jostled him in a lengthy protest. Hewie took the kick and beat Abbes but the ball rebounded from the inside of a post. The frustration of that miss, compounded by a third game peppered with niggling fouling on them, upset the Scottish players' equilibrium. Several Scots became involved in a brawl with the French. Brazzi called the captains together for a stern talking to, and the match resumed.

As half-time approached, Collins' long-range shot again forced

Abbes to make a spectacular save. Then, for the second successive game, the Scots suffered severely in the final seconds of the first half. Jonquet spotted Fontaine in space ahead of him and dropped a long pass into the centre-forward's path. He sped on and sent a measured shot past Brown to give France a daunting 2-0 half-time lead.

Early in the second half Mudie sent a header straight at Abbes when he had time to put the ball either side of the goalkeeper. On 66 minutes, the Scots produced a frisson of finesse. Mackay jabbed the ball forward to Murray. He instantaneously split the French defence with a sharp pass. Baird, on the edge of the 18-yard box, took the ball on the turn and his shot flew into the French net via the foot of a post.

As in the Paraguay game, the Scots put everything into the search for the equalizer. They had, however, to be saved from a decisive French goal when the excellent Brown sprinted from his line to save at Fontaine's feet. The Scots' effort appeared to have been rewarded when Collins put Mudie clear on goal. But he stumbled over the ball, fumbled the chance and, with that, the Scottish World Cup effort was ended for the 1950s.

During the tournament some players had overindulged at the well-stocked restaurant in their hotel. Available were a cooked breakfast and cereal; a three-course meal at lunchtime, and the same at dinnertime. Players also indulged in generous portions of creamy Swedish cakes and sandwiches at the 10 p.m. supper serving. They appeared under no instructions regarding their general conduct – long after supper some players could still be seen lolling in the hotel lounge. Discipline and training appeared, generally, to be lax. Matt Busby's presence had been badly missed by football in the first half of 1958 but nowhere more so than in Eskilstuna in Sweden during June of that year.

Graham Leggat, Scotland's refined outside-right in the 1958 World Cup, challenges England's Billy Wright in a Home International.

MATCHING THE MASTERS

WEST GERMANY, 1974

'Every time you ask this team to get its teeth into something they bite and they bite.'

Willie Ormond

It was a very different World Cup that Scotland looked towards in 1974. In the 1950s most Scots had only a hazy awareness of the tournament's history; by the 1970s that had changed. The two most recent World Cups had, for very different reasons, captured their collective imagination. In 1966, England had won it as hosts, a feat that had stuck in the throats of many Scots fans and players. Then, in 1970, the World Cup in Mexico had been the first to be beamed live around the world by satellite. It had showcased the greatest football team assembled up to that point: Brazil. On the way to winning the trophy, Brazil had played magnificent, inspirational and inspiring football, culminating in a 4-1 dismantling of the Italian defensive machine in the final.

Television coverage, which had been a hit-and-miss affair in the 1950s, was now comprehensive, and by 1974 colour television was becoming widespread, making the spectacle more glamorous and attractive than ever before. The Scots had been confined to their front rooms to watch those televisual spectaculars. Now they wanted a place at the feast.

Scotland now had a full-time manager. Tommy Docherty, after a decade's managerial experience at Chelsea, Rotherham United, Queen's Park Rangers, Aston Villa, Porto and Hull City, had been appointed to the post in October 1971. In the autumn of 1972, his side got off to the perfect start, defeating group rivals Denmark 4-1 in Copenhagen and 2-0 in Glasgow. The other side in the group, however, was Czechoslovakia. They had participated in the 1970 World Cup and looked a far more difficult prospect than the Danes. The home match with the Czechs was scheduled for September 1973.

A month after the second match with Denmark, Manchester United sacked Frank O'Farrell and, on 22 December, Docherty became manager of Manchester United. His annual salary would be £15,000, almost double his salary as Scotland manager.

Docherty, who had been living in Largs, had done a fine job as manager of Scotland, inculcating the winning mentality in the players again. He had worked the trick of getting the Scottish side playing for each other like a good club side. Maintaining a settled selection did much to make that happen. He was well respected and liked by his players, and among those to whom he had given a first cap was Kenny Dalglish. The SFA refused Docherty's request to continue as part-time manager of Scotland. Jock Stein, Celtic's manager, was one of the names mentioned as a possible replacement for Docherty, as were Bill Shankly, manager of Liverpool, and Eddie Turnbull of Hibs.

The new man turned out to be one of Docherty's Scotland colleagues from the 1950s. Willie Ormond's record as manager of St Johnstone in domestic and European competition was impressive but his appointment by the SFA was still a surprise. In contrast to the fast-talking 'Doc', Ormond was almost shy. He was appointed Scotland manager – with an annual salary of £7,500 and a four-year contract – on 5 January

1973. He said: 'Everyone has their own ideas but in this case all I want to do is continue what has been going on under Tommy Doc. The team have been winning respect for Scotland – more respect than we used to have. I will pick the team and be in charge of them just as the Doc was. I'll also be in charge of everything regarding the playing side of the game. I'm sure we can qualify for the World Cup. The games against the Czechs will be hard but we can win them.'

His first match in charge was the centenary international against England at Hampden on 14 February. It was a disaster for Scotland, ending in a 5-0 defeat. By the time of the Czechoslovakia game on 26 September, Ormond's record had improved – but only slightly. After five defeats in six matches he was under pressure. He had done a considerable amount of chopping and changing since taking over. Scotland still had the same problem as in the 1950s – a lack of obvious goalscorers. The Saturday before the Czech match, however, there was sign of a progressive outlook on the part of the Scottish football authorities. Those Scottish clubs with players in the squad for the impending international had their matches postponed.

Denis Law said before the game: 'If I were a Czech I would be worried. Do you think any team fancies playing at Hampden Park knowing that if they lose they are out of the World Cup? Of course not. They are the ones to worry, not us.' While Ormond added: 'Mention the Czechs to my team? Why should I? We'll play our game – there's nothing in their side to worry us at all.'

There were 100,000 at Hampden for the match. Agreement had been reached the day before between Scottish Television and the SFA to televise the match live. If Scotland won, they would become the first European qualifiers for the World Cup. In West Germany, the host country for the 1974 World Cup, the Scotland v Czechoslovakia match was broadcast live.

Denis Law was by then 33 and this would be his 50th cap. There were two new caps in the side: George Connelly of Celtic and Tommy Hutchison of Coventry City. The quiet Connelly was an immensely talented sweeper; Hutchison was an unusually long-legged winger. Peter Lorimer had been one of Scotland's most impressive players against Denmark but he had been sent off against them at Hampden and was now suspended. The team was: Hunter, Jardine, McGrain, Bremner, Holton, Connelly, Morgan, Hay, Law, Dalglish, Hutchison.

Twice in the early stages the Czech goalkeeper Viktor made stunning saves, one from a Bremner header, the second from a powerful Willie Morgan shot. After 32 minutes, Czech striker Nehoda picked the ball up on the right wing. The fans on the North Terrace tottered on tiptoe, craning their necks, suspiciously watching his every move. His eventual action proved deceptively simple, a cross-shot that should have been Hunter's. Instead it flew into the net. Scotland's hard work early in the game had been countered in a flash.

The crowd became anxious; the Scots players continued as though nothing had happened. Viktor saved well from a Law free-kick. Then, in the 40th minute, a piece of simplicity brought the Scots level. Hutchison sent a perfect corner into the heart of the Czech penalty area. Holton rose and thumped a header past Viktor. Midway through the second-half, the foundations were laid for Scotland's presence in Germany in the World Cup finals. A Bremner shot found the foot of a Czech post and went to Morgan on the right. With the Czech defence turning this way and that, the winger steered the ball into the air. Joe Jordan, on as substitute for Dalglish, headed it soundly past Viktor for a goal that sent the whole of Scotland into tumult. Jordan was 21 and was winning only his fourth cap. He had not expected to be even one of the substitutes for this match. It warmed the crowd that both goals had been products of the age-old Scottish skill of achieving powerful accuracy in the air, a skill that, even in the knowing 1970s, the majority of international sides struggled to emulate.

Scotland were in the World Cup finals. Thanks to the unifying powers of TV – still feared and hated by many football officials – few members of the Scottish public would remain untouched by this feat. 'I just can't believe it has happened. That last period seemed to be the longest quarter of an hour of my life. Every 30 seconds I

Willie Ormond, Scotland's manager at the 1974 World Cup, was a quiet, reticent man in public. When hard decisions had to be made with regard to team selections or substitutions, however, he displayed a tough, decisive streak characteristic of all the best managers.

Joe Jordan (centre) steers his header into the Czechoslovakian net in September 1973 for the goal that took Scotland to their first World Cup finals in 16 years. Tommy Hutchison (left) and Denis Law (right) are the Scotland players with a close-up view of one of the most magnificent moments ever enjoyed by Scottish football fans.

checked my watch and the wait seemed never-ending. I also lost my voice shouting at the lads but it was a tremendous victory because the lads did not have the match all their own way. There were times when the Czechs were on top but my team just refused to give up and admit that they would get any result other than a victory,' said Ormond. The crowd stayed on the terraces for 15 minutes at the end, as the players went on a lap of honour. Denis Law called it the greatest victory of his sporting life.

Scotland had six points, the Czechs three. With two points for a win, both sides' final match, when they played each other in Czechoslovakia, was now meaningless. A draw with Denmark had proved costly to the Czechs. Their return with Scotland in Prague ended in a 1-0 Czechoslovakian victory.

Scotland then got down to some serious preparation for the finals. On 14 November, they met West Germany in a friendly at Hampden. It was the third match played that year to celebrate the SFA's centenary – as well as England, Scotland had played Brazil. Lorimer was back after his two-game suspension. David Harvey, the goalkeeper, was making his third appearance. Jordan was again a substitute; this time he came on for Law.

Scotland outplayed the then European champions and World Cup favourites. A headed goal by Holton was the only scoring evidence of that but this performance convinced the near-60,000 present that Scotland had a real chance of doing something in West Germany. Franz Beckenbauer, Uli Hoeness, Gunter Netzer and Berti Vogts were supporting players as the Scots moved the ball around in superb fashion. Bremner had a penalty saved by Sepp Maier before Hoeness plundered a late equalizer. 'You really will be among the favourites next summer. We have known that for some time and the events at Hampden only confirmed our suspicions. It puzzles me that the Scots themselves do not regard themselves in the same way as the rest of the world sees them,' commented Helmut Schoen, the West German manager.

A year to the day after Ormond's appointment as manager, the World Cup draw found Scotland in the most intriguing group for the finals. In Dortmund, on the second

day of the tournament, they would play Zaire, the only African representatives in West Germany. Four days later, on 18 June, they would face world champions Brazil in Frankfurt. On 22 June, again in Frankfurt, they would play Yugoslavia or Spain, who had to meet each other in a play-off for a place in the finals. 'I can see no reason at all why Scotland cannot qualify for the later stages. I am more than happy with the way things have turned out,' said Ormond. 'Brazil are not the team they were. They are having trouble with their team – and the result they gained at Hampden last summer [a 1-0 win] is not important. It was a match we should not have played out of season.'

Scotland would be in the Wald Stadium, Frankfurt, before the tournament for the return friendly with West Germany. Ormond himself would know the stadium like a close relative by the time the World Cup came around – he was also there in February to see Yugoslavia defeat Spain 1-0 in their play-off. The Yugoslavs had been cheered on by thousands of Yugoslavian 'guestworkers' who would be back for the match with Scotland.

In late March, the Scots played West Germany. There were five non-regulars in the Scottish team due to call-offs. The German team was close to the one that would start the World Cup tournament and included six of the Bayern Munich side that would win that season's European Cup. Breitner gave the Germans the lead and Grabowski added to it within a minute. Dalglish scored for Scotland when he broke clear and curved the ball over Maier's body for the best goal of the night. It ended 2-1 to the West Germans but the Scots had been able to match them for patient, skilful football. Among the high points of the match was Martin Buchan's efficient marking job on Gerd Muller, the German striker.

It was Scotland's last warm-up before the Home Internationals in May. In the squad of 22 players for that tournament was one surprise name: Jimmy Johnstone, Celtic's light-footed winger, who had been missing from the international scene for two years. Johnstone had been brought in after a lackadaisical performance from Willie Morgan against West Germany. Gordon McQueen, Leeds United's 21-year-old

Scotland players celebrate the victory over Czechoslovakia with a lap of honour. Captain Billy Bremner is chaired by (from left) Joe Jordan, Danny McGrain, Denis Law, David Hay and Sandy Jardine.

centre-back, as yet uncapped, was also included. Connelly was sadly missing, having suffered a broken ankle in the spring. During this series, David Harvey would become established as the Scotland goalkeeper while Buchan was paired successfully with Holton in central defence.

The Scots were based in Largs while preparing for the Home Internationals. 'My big job now is to see that they do not go stale,' said Ormond. 'After all, this is not the end. It is the beginning of our efforts to bring the World Cup to Scotland.' All three of Scotland's Home Internationals were played in Glasgow: the match with Northern Ireland had been switched from Belfast because of the 'troubles'. In front of 53,000, Scotland played poorly and lost 1-0. In midweek, against Wales, there was some improvement, goals from Dalglish and Jardine making for a satisfactory win. Some Scottish players then enjoyed celebrations that were massively out of proportion to the importance of the game. At 6 a.m., tired of conventional cheer, some players decided to make the most of the Scottish hotel's seaside location and commandeered two rowing boats. Johnstone was alone in one. The others eventually manouevred their way back to the shore but that option was not open to Johnstone: his boat had no rowlocks and began drifting out to sea. He was eventually rescued by a Largs boatman.

Sweeping disciplinary measures appeared out of the question: it was too late for Scotland to even think of replacing the offenders, among whom were some key men. Just over 48 hours later, Johnstone was in the side for the match with England. After their ordinary showings in the two other Home Internationals, it was now important for Scotland to save face. The fixture was almost worthless in football's new international currency but it still meant a great deal to the Scottish fans.

They got what they wished for, a 2-0 win on an emotional afternoon. Scotland had qualified for the World Cup and England had failed to do so; but in most Scottish hearts it was only after this win that they had proved themselves Britain's best international side. Johnstone, rejuvenated by the sea air, was immense. Joe Jordan, a man with the long hair of the 1970s but who appeared to be a traditionalist in his interpretation of the striker's role, didn't give the English defence a minute's peace. He appeared to be one solution to Scotland's goalscoring problems.

Johnstone, on the lap of honour, sent a V-sign in the direction of the press box on the Hampden roof. If this was his response to their criticism it was to be hoped that they would pour gallons of vitriolic ink over him during the coming weeks. Ironically, the Scottish Football Writers' Association had taken the unusual step of naming the 28 players who had played in the World Cup qualifiers against Denmark and Czechoslovakia as the joint winners of the Footballer of the Year award. Journalists were swept away by the nation's optimism – there was a real belief Scotland could reach the final.

The Scottish players recorded a World Cup song – the start of a new tradition. Entitled 'Easy Easy', its hook line was 'Yabba dabba doo, we support the boys in blue and it's easy, easy'. It reached Number 20 in the British charts that June. The going was, however, far from easy, with regard to commercial payments for this and other ventures. In late May, the Scottish players had an unproductive four-hour meeting at Largs with Bob Bain, their business manager. The players had been expecting to receive approximately £10,000 from promotional activities; the figure now seemed likely to be closer to £5,000. Bremner, the Scottish players' representative, was not happy with the situation. (The talented Dutch were also having problems – earlier in the year nine members of their squad had threatened to withdraw from the World Cup in a dispute with their national association over finances.)

On 31 May, Scotland's World Cup squad of 22 flew to Brussels for a friendly with the Belgian national side. Before the match, Ormond said: 'After we beat Zaire, we have to face Brazil, then Yugoslavia. These will be two very hard games. If we can

> *'My big job now is to see that they do not go stale,' said Ormond. 'After all, this is not the end. It is the beginning of our efforts to bring the World Cup to Scotland.'*

qualify from that section, I firmly believe we can go on and win the tournament.'

Holton missed the Belgium game with a knee injury and McQueen was given his first cap. Ormond said he knew his team for the World Cup and that nothing that happened in the two friendlies with Belgium and Norway would change his selection. That took some pressure off his players and allowed them to treat these matches as what they were – high-grade training games. A tepid Saturday night friendly saw Scotland lose 2-1 to Belgium on a bumpy pitch in Bruges. The unreal nature of the affair was emphasized in that it was Kenny Dalglish who gave away the penalty for Belgium's winner close to the end. Johnstone had scored the Scots' goal.

Scotland's hotel in Belgium had been painfully close to a motorway and as they flew to Norway they looked forward to something more peaceful. The contrast was drastic – they found themselves billeted in student accommodation vacated for the use of holidaying families during the summer. Donald Ford described it as 'a glorified youth hostel'. This looked like an SFA cost-saving exercise.

On the evening of their arrival, Bremner and Johnstone took the opportunity to relax into their surroundings with a few drinks in the student bar. After a few more, Johnstone was having a singsong while Bremner was pursuing a fierce argument with a journalist. Willie Ormond, on hearing that Scotland players were becoming boisterous in the bar, made for the scene.

The following day, Willie Allan read a prepared statement: 'On Sunday evening the manager drew the attention of the members of the international committee to an extremely serious breach of discipline on the part of two of the players. The president, chairman of the committee, and the secretary later interviewed the players, who offered profuse apologies and gave an assurance that there would not be a recurrence. In view of this assurance, members of the committee, who had been of the mind to send the players home, decided with some hesitation that they be allowed to stay.'

Sending the players home would have been extraordinarily harsh. The consumption of large amounts of alcohol can never be entirely good for any sportsman. However, drinking has long been an integral part of many British footballers' lives. Even those managers who have disapproved of it have had to come to terms with this. It was unrealistic to expect this to cease simply because there was a World Cup about to happen. The Germans, for example, would regard such behaviour as deeply unprofessional but they would also refrain from drinking heavily throughout their League season. Besides, Johnstone had played one of his best games for Scotland after the Largs rowing-boat incident and the World Cup was still over ten days away. In the succeeding days, Bremner, Johnstone and the other players behaved exceptionally well, establishing a good rapport with the Norwegians in the week that the Scots spent in their country.

Bremner and Johnstone were both in the team that won 2-1 in Norway in another mundane friendly, notable mainly for the performances of Jordan and Dalglish, the goalscorers. Jordan looked extremely sharp, especially in the air, but the victory, overall, owed most to Scotland's superior fitness. Both goals arrived in the final 15 minutes as Norway tired. It seemed unlikely that Scotland's World Cup opponents would be worn down so easily.

The start of a training session three days before the match with Zaire was delayed as Scottish players bargained with a TV crew over the right to film the session. 'I know that the Yugoslavs have a similar row going on,' said Ormond of the players' continued attempts to obtain World Cup cash. 'Brazil have problems too but they keep them quiet. It is only ours that seem to be going on in public.'

On 13 June, Brazil and Yugoslavia kicked off the 1974 World Cup with a stultifying 0-0 draw. The following day, Scotland would face Zaire. Bremner was in confident mood as he looked forward to the tournament: 'I think and I believe we will win. We will take it match by match in the first section. We won't make the mistake of underestimating Zaire because we have been caught that way before. We won't relax either because goals are important all the time. It's only against the English that we like to show our superiority in terms of flashiness. Against the Africans we will play the

British way, hustling and bustling. Then, against Brazil, we must change. If you give them possession you are beaten. So we will keep the ball and be patient. Yugoslavia will be the more difficult as they are physically harder and, unlike the Brazilians, they don't get dispirited when they go a goal behind. After the first round, who knows? But we are going to win this competition or I will want to know the reason why not. We are afraid of no one.'

There were 7,000 Scottish fans in a crowd of 25,000 in the compact Westfalen stadium, newly opened after being built for the World Cup at a cost of 33 million deutschmarks. Zaire were the first African country to take part in the World Cup finals. It was also the first mass visitation on a foreign land of Scotland's travelling support. Even the combative Bremner felt his legs going beforehand due to nerves.

The game was live on both BBC1 and Scottish Television or Grampian – beginning at 7.30 p.m. and part of two-and-a-half hours of live coverage. Later in the evening, there were highlights programmes on both channels. 'If we cannot beat Zaire then we should pack up our bags and go home,' was Ormond's point of view.

In the second minute, as Scotland flew at the Zaireans, Lorimer crossed for Jordan and his header slipped narrowly wide of goal. Midway through the half, a shot from Hay, as Scotland pelted the Zaire defence with shots and headers, made contact with the Zaire post and rebounded into play. In the 27th minute, McGrain crossed and

(top)
Peter Lorimer leans back to sweep a sweet volley into the Zaire net for Scotland's opening goal in the 1974 finals. Kenny Dalglish (extreme left) watches.

(bottom)
Denis Law shoots for goal against Zaire. It was to be Law's 55th and final cap for Scotland – after this match Willie Ormond made the firm but fair decision to replace him with Willie Morgan. Law, then 34 years old, retired from international football after the 1974 finals as Scotland's all-time top scorer with 30 goals.

Jordan intelligently nodded the ball back to Lorimer on the edge of the penalty area. Balanced like a ballet dancer, he swiped a volley past Kazadi, the Zaire goalkeeper.

Eight minutes later, Bremner's free-kick found Jordan, unmarked and in space in front of goal. He got a header on target but it was a powerless effort and it was directed straight at Kazadi. The goalkeeper bent to claim the ball but it escaped his grasp and inched over the line to make the score 2-0 to Scotland. But Zaire failed to play the expected role and collapse. Playing 4-2-4, they went after a goal and, following several near things, Harvey was forced to save bravely at the feet of Kidumu as he readied himself to shoot.

After an hour of the match, a five-minute floodlight failure interrupted proceedings and when play resumed the light was at half-power. On a humid night, Scotland became more and more wearied by the heat. With Zaire hurtling at them, Bremner told his team-mates to calm things down and retain possession rather than become caught up in the unpredictabilities of cup-tie football. For the final 20 minutes the Scots played keep-ball.

Zaire had further chances and were unlucky not to get at least one goal. It was Scotland, however, who came nearest to changing the 2-0 scoreline. Close to the end, a Lorimer shot streaked off a Zaire post. It was, without doubt, a good result, a result Scotland could build on. There was one niggling tactical error: the Scots had started

Billy Bremner, an inspirational captain at the 1974 World Cup, runs at the Zaire defence. Now 32, Bremner, like Law, realised this was his last chance of making an impact on the World Cup and he did so, winning over admirers such as Pelé.

Willie Ormond leaves the Scotland World Cup team bus prior to a training session for the match with Brazil.

Scotland fans mingle peaceably with their Brazilian counterparts before the match in Frankfurt. The 1974 World Cup found the Scots fans in excellent form and at subsequent World Cups they have mixed
happily with opposition fans and locals alike.

the game without wingers. Yet throughout the game they had employed high balls in seeking Jordan and Law in an attempt to exploit the Zaireans' weakness in the air. Both goals came as a result of crosses. With one or two wingers reaching the goal-line and turning defenders while getting crosses in, this tactic might have been more effective.

For the first time, Scotland had won a World Cup finals match; it was also the first time they had topped their group in the finals. After the first round of matches, Scotland, West Germany, Holland and Italy were the four group leaders.

Before the match with Brazil, regular TV bulletins monitored the progress of the Scotland team and their fans. In the evening, the dedicated watcher could see four-and-a-half hours of World Cup football with Scotland v Brazil live on both BBC and STV. BBC 2 screened the film, *The Bad and the Beautiful.* Scotland were never likely to be clearly one or the other but this Brazilian side were contributing a degree of badness to the game their erstwhile star Pelé had once described as beautiful.

A two-day trip to the Brazil match, including flights from Glasgow and hotel accommodation, was priced at £50. British Prime Minister Harold Wilson opted to take a helicopter to the Wald stadium. World champion racing drivers Jackie Stewart, a Scot, and Emerson Fittipaldi, a Brazilian, went to the game together. Sir Alf Ramsey, who had recently relinquished his post as England manager, peeked over the balcony of his hotel in downtown Frankfurt at the tartan-covered fans. He was greeted with an enormous cheer.

Willie Ormond met Jock Stein for a tactical discussion on the Brazil game. Brazilian coach Mario Zagallo said: 'We hope that Scotland play football and do not make war.' Brazil had had a three-month preparation period during which their players had played only international matches.

It was another muggy evening for the match at the Wald stadium, which had been completely refurbished for the 1974 World Cup. All 63,000 tickets had been sold. Before the game, every Scottish player went to the fans around the ground and presented one chosen fan with a red rose. The Scottish team then unfurled a West German flag. In their first game, the German fans had taken the side of the underdogs, Zaire. This time the Scots hoped to engage their sympathies. Ten thousand Scottish fans greeted 'God Save the Queen' in the only way they knew how. 'It's absolutely ridiculous that a Scottish hymn isn't played before the game,' said Willie Ormond afterwards. 'It's embarrassing when we play abroad, especially for the players, when the fans react in this way. I'm not blaming them or even disapproving of their resentment. In fact, I think it's high time we had our own Scottish national anthem. We are here representing Scotland – not England, Ireland or Wales. It's Scotland we're playing for – no one else.' The SFA line was that Scotland were representing Britain.

Against Zaire, Law had been unable to contribute much to the game. He was missing from the Scotland side that faced Brazil. The only other change was Buchan for Blackley in the centre of the Scottish defence. Brazilian 'banana kicks' were all the rage in the 1970s and Nelinho, Brazil's right-back, unpeeled one immed-iately. It bent out then in as it approached Harvey's goal but slipped wide of the post. Lorimer responded with a free-kick that was on target but was saved by goalkeeper Leão.

Rivelino hammered in a shot; Harvey pushed it round his post. From Nelinho's corner, left-winger Levinha turned quickly on the ball and battered it past Harvey but against the Scotland bar. Rivelino, showing the new face of Brazil, was booked for a foul on Bremner. The Brazilians were becoming frustrated and the game fell into a trough before half-time. The last significant action of the half came from Scotland. A Lorimer shot from outside the penalty area swerved beautifully in mid-air but followed a route over the Brazilian bar. Shortly after half-time, another long-range shot took Scotland closer to the breakthrough. Bremner, working away in midfield like a Highland Terrier, prodded the ball on to the impressive Hay. He directed a shot towards goal that dipped under Leão's bar but the goalkeeper managed to push it over.

> *'It's Scotland we're playing for – no one else.'*

Lorimer's resultant corner was headed downwards by Jordan but Leão held on to the ball tightly. Another Hay shot, and one from Lorimer, kept Leão busy. Lorimer's best effort of the match, a 25-yard twister, was tipped over by Leão. Just as the Brazilian tradition of fluid football had been traded for a spoiling game, so Leão was doing his best to disprove the dictum that Brazilian goalkeepers were always incompetent.

With 20 minutes remaining, another Scottish move fully examined the Brazilians. Lorimer's corner was headed on to Bremner by Jordan. Only a few yards from goal, Leão dived at Bremner's feet as the Scottish captain prepared to shoot. For once the ball eluded the Brazilian but he had done just enough to unsettle Bremner and the shot skirted the Brazilian post by centimetres. Lorimer tested Leão with another fierce free-kick, then a Jordan header was stopped by the goalkeeper's legs. Brazil had no response to Scotland's invention but when the final whistle went they had eked out a valuable draw.

Billy Bremner's shot squeezes just the wrong side of the Brazilian post as Scotland attempt to get the goal that would reflect their overall dominance of Brazil in this match.

*Joe Jordan (hidden) is con-
gratulated warmly by Jim
Holton (left), Billy Bremner
(centre) and Sandy Jardine
(right) after scoring the
equalizer against Yugoslavia.*

'Ours is by far the toughest group. While we had to face two strong teams in Yugoslavia and Scotland the West Germans have had an easy time,' said Zagallo. He also accused the Scots of rough play. 'If he thinks that, he should come down to our dressing room and look at the shins of my players. There is hardly a man unmarked. Brazil came to play European-type football in this World Cup. It is against their natural game. They can't do it and this is why they tackle so crudely,' responded Ormond. 'I am a tremendous admirer of Rivelino but after he was booked he had another three bad fouls which should have brought him the red card. He should have been off the field.' Close to the end of the game, Rivelino had punched Bremner full in the face. Pelé said: 'Bremner may turn out to be the best player in this World Cup. He is an inspiration to his side, a free organizer and the outstanding improviser and leader of men of all the countries.'

Ormond was satisfied with the evening's work: 'With a little luck we could have won. If my boys can turn in the same performance as tonight – and are given a break – I think they can beat Yugoslavia.' The Scottish players partied into the night after the game against Brazil on the Tuesday night. Their next game would be with Yugoslavia on the following Saturday afternoon. 'Sure, Yugoslavia are a helluva team but weren't we against Brazil? Every time you ask this team to get its teeth into something they bite and they bite. I'll be asking once again and they'll do it for me,' said Ormond.

There was much talk about the player-power of the independently minded Dutch during this tournament but Ormond also had to compromise to deal with it. 'These players are great people,' he said. 'They told me how they wanted to play the game against Brazil, with Morgan and Lorimer wide, Dalglish up among the attack. In my heart I knew it wasn't on but I said, "OK, we'll give it 20 minutes the way you want it, you are the ones that count." It didn't work, as I knew it wouldn't, but you have to respect and listen to the opinions of players. The style was changed with Lorimer going inside and Dalglish coming back. But I didn't have to say a word, the captain and the others worked it out for themselves. I'm proud of them for that and didn't they play well afterwards?'

Scotland were based at the Hotel Erbismuhle in the Taunus Mountains. They were surrounded by armed security men, as they had been since they had stepped off the plane from Norway at Frankfurt airport. Now, the day before the match with Yugoslavia, they received a jolt. A letter, purporting to be from an Irish Republican terrorist organization, containing a threat to kill two unnamed Protestant members of the Scottish squad, was received. Security was stepped up, with players being kept inside the hotel. Conditions became more relaxed when the IRA officially said they had nothing to do with the threat.

Around 12,000 Scots were in Frankfurt the weekend of the Yugoslavia match but they were outnumbered in the 55,000 crowd by 35,000 Yugoslavs. The two sides' first-choice colours were almost identical so there was a toss-up for colours before-hand. Scotland would play in white.

'Matches don't come any bigger than this one and again they will rise to the occasion. Sure it's difficult. Yugoslavia break so quickly and so well that sometimes they give you no time to regroup. They remain one of the favourites for the World Cup but then we will be among the favourites if we can get this match over. There will be no more difficult game in the later stages. In fact it will be easier,' said Ormond.

Yugoslavia had beaten Zaire 9-0 to equal the World Cup finals' goalscoring record. That put the Yugoslavs top of the group. Each team knew what they had to do. Yugoslavia needed only a draw to be sure of qualifying while Brazil needed to beat Zaire by at least three clear goals. Scotland required a win to be absolutely sure of going into the next round.

The match kicked off at 4 p.m. and was accommodated live in extended editions of Grandstand and World of Sport, Independent Television's Saturday afternoon sports programme. Before the game, Yugoslavia's coach Milan Miljanic said: 'This is the best team that we have ever had. Not just the 11 who will play but 18 and maybe all 22 of the squad cannot be bettered.' That was a harsh thought for Scots who appreciated good football; the Yugoslavs were traditionally excellent ball-players.

It was a tight, tense game. Scotland, with Bremner again dominant, constantly equalled the Yugoslavs in terms of technical excellence. The two teams matched each other's moves with cat-like stealth. Chances were scarce but Scotland had the clearest one of the first half. Jardine, the Scots' outstanding player on the day, had a shot blocked by Katalinski. Jordan took hold of the ball but Maric, the Yugoslavian goal-keeper, was quick to block his scoring effort.

In the second half, Jordan did well to find space in behind the Yugoslavian defence but he failed to get any power on his header after Bremner had sent a free-kick in his direction. With eight minutes of the match remaining, Karasi knocked the ball to Dzajic on the wing. The Yugoslavian captain took it on, then returned the favour. As his cross came gliding over, Karasi raced into position, adjusted his body and dived to head a splendid goal.

In the final minute, Hutchison took a pass from Hay and went careering down the left wing with his distinctive, broken, loping stride. He hit a low cross deep into the Yugoslavian six-yard box. Lorimer went for it but couldn't make proper contact. The ball jerked towards Jordan who knocked it into the air, then sidefooted it past five

Kenny Dalglish eases on to the ball against Yugoslavia. Dalglish, then 23 years old, worked hard for the Scottish team in the 1974 World Cup but was unable to reproduce the subtle, individualistic skills he had shown so often at club level.

Joe Jordan gets in among the Yugoslavian defenders. Jordan was Scotland's most feared striker of the 1970s because of his ability in the air, his controlled aggression and his fearlessness. He could score goals but was also extremely unselfish in creating opportunities for others.

Yugoslavs and into the net at the far post. It produced a double somersault of celebration from Bremner. He knew Brazil were beating Zaire 2-0. If the scores remained the same, Scotland would have an identical goal difference to Brazil but the Scots would claim second place in the group on the basis of having scored more goals.

On reaching their dressing room the Scottish players discovered that there were three minutes left in the match between Brazil and Zaire. Three minutes later they heard that Valdomiro had scored a third goal for Brazil in the final minute of their match. It was the flukiest of goals too. Scotland were out by the narrowest possible margin.

After the game, Miljanic said: 'Willie Ormond came into the dressing-room afterwards and congratulated us. Nothing finer will happen in the tournament. You are the greatest sportsmen in the world and good, good players.' On Monday 24 June there were 10,000 Scottish fans at Glasgow airport to welcome the team home.

In the years that followed, it was lamented that Scotland had gone out because they had failed to build up their goal difference in the match with Zaire. This was a red herring. That game had been a tough one and it was patronizing to the Africans to suggest otherwise. Zaire had themselves come close to scoring. With a bit of luck, the way the game went, the best Scotland could have come away with would have been a 4-0 or 5-0 victory. Had that happened, Brazil would simply have been set a higher goalscoring target against Zaire in their final game. The Africans would by then have been reeling from letting in nearly 15 goals in their first two games. Under those circumstances, it would be highly unlikely that Brazil would fail to obtain the necessary quota of goals. It is worth noting that after the 9-0 defeat to Yugoslavia the Africans were so upset that they were on the point of scratching from the tournament: two massive defeats in their first two games would have left them totally demoralized.

The other misleading statistic was that Scotland had unluckily been the only

unbeaten side in the World Cup and yet had gone out. But at the end of that first group stage, East Germany, Holland, Sweden, Brazil, Yugoslavia and Poland were also unbeaten. The difference was that they all went on to the tougher final group stage. Scotland's result against Zaire, all things considered, was fine. Their weakness was in failing to beat either Brazil or Yugoslavia. They knew before each of those games that a win would take them into the next round – they failed to obtain it. Drawing each of those games suited their opponents perfectly. Possessing the nerve to obtain wins at such moments is a vital part of the make-up of the very best international sides.

Scotland could now claim to be the ninth-best international side in the world. That was no mean achievement for a country that had spent a decade and a half in the international wilderness. They had been knocked out at a point when – with real justification – their self-belief was growing. There was still cause for optimism: most of this squad would still be in their prime by the time of the next World Cup – in Argentina in 1978.

Willie Morgan gets his balance right against Yugoslavia as Scotland seek a route into the last eight of the 1974 World Cup.

ALLY'S ARMY

ARGENTINA, 1978

'The players and myself decided before the match to say "To hell with everyone" and play as we can play.'

Ally MacLeod after Scotland v Holland

at the 1978 World Cup

A match with the Czechs at Hampden would once more prove the key to qualification in Scotland's World Cup campaign of 1978. They would again go into this match with a new manager, one who, as in 1973, had been appointed just a few months previously, after the previous incumbent had quit to take up an attractive offer with a club side.

On 6 May 1977, the SFA accepted Willie Ormond's resignation from the post of Scotland manager. He said he wished to keep more normal working hours as the new manager of Hearts. His final duty in charge of Scotland was to name a squad for the Home Internationals and Scotland's tour of South America in June. The SFA wanted Jock Stein as his replacement but Stein had just won the double with Celtic, and with Kenny Dalglish and Danny McGrain as his mainstays was looking to a bright future with the club.

With six matches fast approaching, the SFA felt the need to make a swift appointment. On 18 May, Ally MacLeod, manager of Aberdeen, became manager of Scotland. MacLeod had shown impressive skills when in charge of Ayr United. After moving on to Aberdeen, he had, in just over a year, helped them win the Scottish League Cup, the Dons' first trophy in six years, and turned them into serious title contenders. He was known for his loquaciousness: on Boxing Day 1976 the Celtic fans regaled the visiting Aberdeen manager with the chant 'Ally, Ally, Shut Your Mouth, Ally, Shut Your Mouth'.

'I want to prove I am the best manager in the world,' was how he saw his new role. 'People might laugh but I firmly believe I was born to be a success.' The 46-year-old MacLeod would be on an annual salary of £15,000. He had worked without a contract at Aberdeen and would do the same with Scotland, such was his self-belief.

After a 0-0 draw in Wales in the opening match of the Home Internationals, Kenny Dalglish scored the first goal of the MacLeod era in a 3-0 win over Northern Ireland at Hampden.

Scotland then faced England at Wembley on 4 June. Before the game MacLeod said: 'Being over-confident could be a danger. All right, we feel good now, but we must come down to earth. Wembley is another ball-game.' It proved a thunderous, fiery victory over England such as the Scottish fans love to see. A Gordon McQueen header and a gritty goal from Dalglish gave them a thoroughly convincing 2-1 win. After the Wembley game few Scots felt anything other than optimism for the future of a team with a fluid, exciting style of play. Scotland had a strong defence, intelligent, creative midfielders and dynamic forwards. MacLeod received boundless praise. He played it down: 'Much tougher battles are to be faced. We still have a lot to do. But we have a magnificent squad.'

In South America, after a 4-2 win in Chile, the Scots faced the following year's World Cup hosts, an Argentina side that included Ardiles, Passarella, Luque and Houseman. They also had a Killer at left-back. The 1-1 draw was one of the least amicable friendlies in Scotland's international history – winger Willie Johnston was sent off in tears with Pernia, who had spat on and punched him. A 2-0 defeat in Brazil ended the tour.

Three months later, on 21 September, the Czechs came to Hampden. The capacity, because of new safety regulations, was limited to 85,000 and those tickets had all been sold weeks previously. The Czechs asked for a 24-hour postponement after their nightmare journey to Scotland. They had had no option but to travel from London on an overnight train, sleeping on upright seats, because all sleeper accommodation was already fully booked. Their flight from Prague had been delayed by three hours so they had missed their connecting London-Glasgow plane. And, to cap it all, staff at their hotel in Erskine staged a 24-hour walkout over general working conditions.

The Czechs were, at the time, Europe's top international side. They had won the 1976 European Championship, defeating West Germany in the final in Yugoslavia.

Ally MacLeod (centre) guided Scotland to the 1978 World Cup finals with memorable wins over Czechoslovakia and Wales. In contrast to Willie Ormond, his predecessor, MacLeod was always jovial and gave the appearance of being light-hearted.

They did not get their postponement and, at the appointed time, faced this Scotland side: Rough, Jardine, McGrain, Forsyth, McQueen, Rioch, Masson, Dalglish, Jordan, Hartford, Johnston. 'This is the one we have all been waiting for,' said MacLeod. 'It will be exciting, with plenty of goalmouth incidents and our crowd could lift the team to great heights. We must open out in an effort to get goals.' The players were true to his words.

Kenny Dalglish signalled the start of proceedings when he struck a shot that crept past the post. Masson's effort from just outside the penalty area was stopped by Michalik, the Czech goalkeeper. After intense Scottish pressure the Czech barriers finally broke on 18 minutes. Blue jerseys flooded the Czech penalty area as Willie Johnston teed the ball up at a corner. The left-winger crossed from right to left and as the ball sailed to the edge of the six-yard box Joe Jordan repeated history by leaping to smack a header into the Czech net. On 35 minutes, Johnston, on the left wing, sent over another high cross. Jordan, Michalik and centre-back Dvorak went for it and collided in mid-air. The ball fell free. Asa Hartford swiftly shuffled his feet and sidefooted it into the unguarded goal.

Nine minutes after half-time, Scotland sealed the win. Masson's corner was headed goalwards by Jardine and Dalglish twisted on to it to spin a header past Michalik. Gajdusek made it 3-1 near the end, but as the fans left Hampden they were fully satisfied that Scotland would be returning to Argentina in 1978. It had been a display of skill and high-speed precision in all aspects of the game; the consummate committed Scottish performance. A win in their final match, with Wales, would take them to the World Cup finals. If they played as they had done against the Czechs that would be a certainty.

The commitment of the Scottish supporters had caused its problems. 'Even when a team-mate shouted from about five yards away you couldn't hear him. I am so glad for the public that we won. They have stood behind us all the way,' said the Scottish captain Bruce Rioch. For ten minutes after the final whistle, the crowd stood and chanted MacLeod's name. Neither he nor the team re-emerged to take a bow. 'This was not an occasion for the team manager appearing or for the team coming back out for a lap of honour. There is still the important qualifying match against Wales to be faced. But if the fans get behind us at Liverpool like this and we get this kind of result, then it will be very different. The whole team was brilliant. The Scottish World Cup pool is sound and I have not got a weakness. Our team showed class tonight,' said MacLeod. Willie Ormond had come into the dressing-room after the match to congratulate the team and the new manager.

The Welsh match had been switched to Anfield to accommodate the expected crowd. Scotland had beaten Wales 1-0 at Hampden in the autumn of 1976, while again the Czechs had faltered against the weakest side in the group, losing 3-0 in Wales.

The players who got tremendous backing from the 30,000 Scots in a 50,850 crowd at Anfield were: Rough, Jardine, Donachie, Forsyth, McQueen, Masson, Macari, Hartford, Dalglish, Jordan, Johnston. Early in the game a series of chances had come Scotland's way but they were squandered. The Welsh weren't too enterprising but they stopped Scotland from being creative, and with the score still 0-0 in the second half Toshack got the opportunity Wales had hoped would fall their way. With only Rough to beat, he extended a leg to lob the ball towards goal. Rough, stretching backwards, diverted the ball on to the bar and over for a corner.

In the 78th minute of a tight, hard-fought game, Jordan and Dave Jones of Wales jumped for Willie Johnston's throw-in. French referee Robert Wurtz pointed to the penalty spot, having adjudged that Jones had handled the ball. Don Masson, the Scotland captain in place of the injured Rioch, parked the ball neatly in the back of the Welsh net. Nine minutes later, Buchan, on as a substitute for Jardine, swept into inviting space down the right wing and angled a neat cross forward, to drop at head-height at the near post. Kenny Dalglish, with characteristic deftness, arced the ball over Welsh goalkeeper Dai Davies' head. It was a magnificent way for Dalglish to celebrate

Joe Jordan (opposite) in the thick of the action against Wales at Anfield. An aerial tussle between Jordan and Dave Jones of Wales resulted in Scotland being awarded the penalty that put them firmly on course for the 1978 World Cup. The French referee adjudged that Jones had handled the ball while challenging Jordan inside the Welsh penalty area.

Don Masson directs the ball smoothly past Welsh goal-keeper Dai Davies for the 78th minute penalty that sent Anfield into a tartan tumult and left Scotland just 12 minutes away from reaching the finals in Argentina.

his 50th cap. Scotland were the first European qualifiers for the World Cup finals.

Don Masson stated that he believed Scotland would win the World Cup and that most of his Scotland squad-mates felt the same. 'There is a tremendous optimism in the squad just now,' he told Alex Cameron of the *Daily Record*. 'We know we can play the game and we want to show the world just how well we can play. The draw will be important. If it favours us at all then we can go on to do what we all want to do – win the World Cup.'

At 9 p.m. on 14 January 1978 the draw, made in Buenos Aires' Teatro San Martin, could be seen on a *Scotsport Special*. Rioch, Masson, Derek Johnstone, McGrain and Rough were in the studio to provide their comments. Scotland were drawn with Holland, who, in reaching the final in 1974, had proved themselves the finest international side Europe had produced up until then. They were unbeaten in six qualifying games with Belgium, Northern Ireland and Iceland. Scotland would also play Peru, quarter-finalists in 1970 and second to Brazil in their South American qualifying group, and Iran, unbeaten in 12 qualifying games. MacLeod, in Buenos Aires with Ernie Walker for the draw, said: 'The draw gives us a good chance, especially as we have Peru and Iran first. I did not want to play the seeded side first, no matter what group we were in.' Rioch added: 'It is a marvellous draw. We play Peru and Iran first, so we could be through to the last eight before we meet Holland.'

For a friendly against Bulgaria in February, Masson and Rioch were injured so MacLeod named Archie Gemmill as his captain. Graeme Souness, winning his fourth cap, was the other midfield replacement. Aberdeen defenders Stuart Kennedy and Willie Miller and Coventry City goalkeeper Jim Blyth also played in this match. A crowd of 58,000 paid between £1 for uncovered terracing and £3 for the stand. Goals from Gemmill and another new cap, striker Ian Wallace of Coventry City, gave Scotland a 2-1 win. Wallace, who came on as a substitute for Dalglish, was making his debut. He took his goal – a shot on the run – well, while Gemmill was outstanding. On a night of pouring rain, it was another suave, accomplished Scotland performance.

In early May, MacLeod named his squad of 22 for the World Cup. It contained a preponderance of midfield players, so the choice of strikers had to be right. There were only four in the pool: Dalglish, Johnstone, Jordan and Joe Harper. The final striker's position had gone to Harper in preference to Wallace and Andy Gray of Aston Villa, a man who had achieved the rare feat of being voted Player of the Year and Young

Kenny Dalglish (left), the scorer of Scotland's second goal against Wales and Don Masson, Scotland's captain, celebrate inside Anfield after Scotland's 2-0 victory. The Welsh had switched their home tie from their own country to Anfield to maximise the revenue from the expected invasion of Scottish fans. They were rewarded with a capacity crowd but the massed Scottish support helped to urge their men on to the win.

Player of the Year in England in 1977. Gray was still raw at international level; in 1976 he had been sent off in the first World Cup qualifier away to Czechoslovakia. Wallace, however, could consider himself extremely unlucky to have been discarded after scoring on his brief appearance against Bulgaria. The 30-year-old Harper had won just three caps – two in 1972, one in 1975, all against Denmark. The only clue to his selection was that MacLeod had relied heavily on him during his club days at Aberdeen. He had also been one of the 'Copenhagen Five' who had been banned, supposedly for life, by the SFA after an incident in a nightclub at the time of the Denmark match in 1975. MacLeod said that Gray and Johnstone were both left-sided players and that Johnstone's superior strength in the air meant he would be included as cover for Jordan.

MacLeod seemed sure of his selection: 'I know exactly how we'll play in every type of situation. I know the men I'll use. Naming the final squad was the hardest part but I have chosen the people who can do the right job for Scotland. That's it, so I stand or fall on what these 22 men do or do not do in South America. Scotland's great strength is in the midfield. We have an abundance of talent in that department, so why not take that talent with us? The entire pool is based on the midfield. It is also an attacking pool. Only three men, apart from the goalkeepers, are out-and-out defenders – Martin Buchan, Kenny Burns and Tom Forsyth. Even the three full-backs are attack-minded.'

Kenny Burns was England's Player of the Year; Johnstone was Scotland's Player of the Year. Other members of the Scottish squad were not faring so well. In November 1977, Tommy Docherty, now manager of Derby County, had signed Rioch and Masson for his midfield. In the month the Scotland squad was announced, Docherty put both players on the transfer list. Rioch 30, and Masson, 32, had been out of form since joining Derby.

Scotland were seen as serious contenders for the World Cup: Ladbrokes announced that Scotland were 8-1 to win the trophy. The entire country seemed to share this belief: this year witnessed the first mass explosion of Scotland replica shirts. A short-sleeved Scotland shirt cost £4.70, shorts were £1.75, socks £1.20.

MacLeod stated that he would not play his chosen 11 for the World Cup in any of the three Home International matches. Instead, he would be experimenting in every area of the field. He maintained that by playing almost all of his squad, players would not become complacent and think they were guaranteed a place in the team. A crowd of 64,433 turned up at Hampden for the first game of the series, again a match that was nominally Northern Ireland's home game. A firm header by Johnstone, from Rioch's cross, was the best thing about the 1-1 draw.

On 15 May Rod Stewart paid a regal visit to the Scots' headquarters at Dunblane Hydro to wish them success. He had recorded the official Scotland World Cup song with the Scottish national squad, the samba-styled 'Ole Ola'. It reached Number 4 in the British charts and featured the tortuous rhyme 'Ole Ola, We're gonna bring that World Cup back from over tha'. Another song, more from the Scottish music-hall tradition, 'Ally's Tartan Army', by Scottish entertainer Andy Cameron, told of how we were on the march with Ally's Army. It promised to 'really shake them up, when we win the World Cup'. It made Number 6.

'Ole Ola, We're gonna bring that World Cup back from over tha'

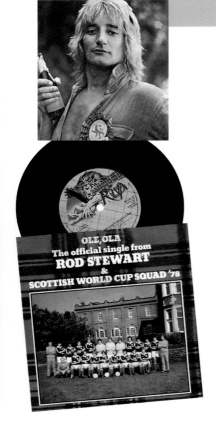

Against Wales, there were 70,000 at Hampden on a Wednesday night. An exceptional header by Johnstone, from Gemmill's right-wing cross, put Scotland ahead in the first half. But in the final seconds of the match Willie Donachie overhit a back pass and watched the ball sail into his own net. A more significant hurt happened to Gordon McQueen: he collided with a goalpost when making a goal-line clearance. He had damaged knee ligaments. It was doubtful whether he would be able to play in any of the opening three World Cup games but he would still make the trip to Argentina in the hope that he would be fit in the event of Scotland making the latter stages of the tournament. A long-term ankle injury had, months previously, seen McGrain ruled out of the World Cup.

MacLeod and his players watched Peru on video during the Home Internationals. McLeod said: 'We watched Peru lose 3-1 to Argentina on television and I must say I was impressed. They were unlucky to lose by two goals and they showed that they are a strong side going forward. They are geared for attack and they are also a very physical side.'

A crowd of 88,000 saw Scotland play England off the park in the final Home International but lose 1-0. The Scottish fans, who know a moral victory when they see one, stood and cheered on the terraces for 25 minutes, demanding that MacLeod and the players return to take a bow, which they eventually did.

On Thursday 25 May, in the early evening, a crowd of 25,000 assembled at Hampden Park. There was no football match taking place. Instead, the Scotland squad made its farewell appearance. The players, wearing £100 SFA suits, were introduced by Andy Cameron as they made individual entrances via a guard of honour consisting of 80 of the Merrylee Drum Majorettes and the Barmulloch Majorettes. Each girl sported a Scottish standard. Then the entire squad drove round the running track, twice, in an open-topped bus. A 40-minute TV programme entitled *Argentina Here We Come!* captured the excitement.

Another guard of honour greeted the Scots party when they arrived in Argentina. Students in the Argentinian national costume made an archway of lances as the Scots disembarked from the plane. They were also greeted by a handful of Scottish fans who had flown to New York at a stand-by price of £65 – a direct flight to Argentina from Britain cost £907 in economy class – and then hitch-hiked to Argentina. (Argentina was at that time ruled by a military junta with an atrocious human rights record and a pamphlet issued by tour operators advised Scottish fans travelling there not to carry guns, to stay out of military 'no-go' areas and to be well insured for medical treatment.)

'We all have our job to do and that is to win the World Cup for Scotland. Nothing must be allowed to interfere with that,' said Rioch on arrival. With a week to go before the first match, against Peru, there was a danger of boredom setting in. 'Saturday cannot come quickly enough for all of us. We are here to play football and the sooner the better,' said MacLeod at Scotland's hotel at Alta Gracia. And he told Alex Cameron of the *Daily Record* a week before kick-off against Peru: 'We are here to win the World Cup, not friends. Dunblane was a shambles when we were preparing for the Home Internationals. Our training was being constantly interrupted. This won't happen here. I'm not going to say the Peru game is the be-all and end-all. I know the players think it is the vital one, but there are three games and we want to win them all. One game is as important as the other. I still think we will get a medal.'

Four days before the match, Marcus Calderon, Peru's manager, said: 'While the Scots have a strong defence I do not think they are flexible enough. Peru will play short, possession football. We will play on the ground, frustrate Scotland and finally wear them down.' Calderon had strong motivation to do well. In April he had travelled to Italy in the belief that he was going to see the Scottish national side in action. On arrival he discovered he would be watching a team representing the Scottish League. The cash-strapped Peruvian FA had barely been able to afford the money to send him to Italy and when news of his abortive trip got out he became an object of ridicule in Peru. A win over Scotland would restore his reputation.

Julio Melendez of Peru said: 'I think Scotland are in for a shock from the "has-beens and old men of Peru". Although Cubillas, Chumpitaz and Ramirez were involved in the World Cup finals in Mexico in 1970 we also have good young players such as Oblitas, Rojas and Quesada.'

Before the action started, Ernst Happel, Holland's manager, said: 'It is Holland and Scotland to qualify from Group 4. We look on the matches against Peru and Iran as practice games. Our final group match with Scotland will be the big one. We both should have already qualified by then but the big problem then for us is that we want to avoid Brazil in the second round. So we would have to go all out to beat the Scots.'

Both BBC and STV broadcast three-hour programmes centred on the match. Few of Scotland's 5 million inhabitants would have missed the coverage, such was the hype. New, large-screen televisions were being advertised – with 8ft screens – for pubs to show the World Cup.

In front of 46,000 in Cordoba, Scotland sprang immediately into action. Hartford's pass opened up a chance for Dalglish after two minutes but his shot was saved by Quiroga. Two minutes later, a Masson strike was stopped dead by Quiroga. In the tenth minute, Dalglish and Hartford combined forces to create another chance for Masson but his shot was again well held by Quiroga.

Scotland were looking good. They were linking well with each other, at an exceptional pace. It was, however, important that they got a goal in return for their impressive start. It was unlikely they'd be able to stay in control throughout the match. Peru

Joe Jordan (left) celebrates with Stuart Kennedy (centre) and Asa Hartford (right) after getting Scotland off to the best possible start in the 1978 World Cup finals with the opening goal against Peru.

would surely have their moments. After 14 minutes, Johnston found Dalglish who quickly passed to Hartford. His swift thinking gave Rioch space for a firm shot that Quiroga parried. It rolled away from the goalkeeper and Joe Jordan sprinted smartly to knock the ball into the net for a neatly taken goal.

Peru retaliated hard and fast, putting the Scottish defence under severe pressure. Rough had to make several demanding saves and the Scots were finding it difficult to get out of their own half. Two minutes from half-time, Rough was finally beaten when, after some intricate Peruvian footwork inside the Scottish penalty area, Cueto shot under the goalkeeper's body from the edge of the six-yard box.

The Scots looked in better shape after half-time. Jordan had a header tipped over the bar by Quiroga and on 62 minutes further Scottish pressure told. Rioch was brought down by Diaz in the penalty box and Ulf Eriksson, the Swedish referee, awarded the penalty. Masson prepared to restore Scotland's lead from the spot but he failed to give it his best shot and his kick was saved by Quiroga. Peru made the most of their reprieve. Eight minutes later, Cubillas took the ball to the edge of the Scottish penalty area and bent an astonishing shot past the Scottish defenders and inside Rough's right-hand post.

In the 77th minute Kennedy tripped Oblitas just outside the penalty area to give away a free-kick. It was to be taken from a similar position and distance from where Cubillas had put Peru into the lead. He repeated his earlier performance, swerving the ball round the Scottish defensive wall and past Rough.

> 'We have to treat the next two matches like Bannockburn, for nothing less than victory over Iran and Holland will do.'

As the Scottish team sat in the dressing-room, demoralized by the 3-1 defeat, Willie Johnston and Kenny Dalglish were picked to have doping samples taken. Johnston's proved positive. FIFA stated that Fencamfamin – 'a psycho-motor stimulant' – had been found in Johnston's sample. Johnston admitted he had taken two pills called Reactivan, prescribed for him by a doctor in Britain. He said he had had hay fever since arriving in Argentina and that he only took the pills when feeling 'low'. The SFA had stressed to the players that they had to inform the team doctor if they were taking any substances. Johnston said he hadn't informed the SFA because he didn't realize there was a problem with these pills.

Fencamfamin was listed by FIFA as a banned stimulant drug. It was used for treating fatigue and not an ailment like hay fever. It was a pick-me-up that would sharpen awareness and the senses although it wouldn't directly improve physical performance. It made the Peru result irrelevant. Had Scotland won, the result would have been reversed by FIFA. Luckily for Johnston, the team had lost.

On 5 June, the SFA told Johnston he was being sent home and that he would never play for Scotland again. The association knew that FIFA had the power to eject Scotland from the World Cup so the SFA had to be seen to take strong action. After due consideration, FIFA banned Johnston from international football for one year. He had been only the second World Cup footballer found guilty of taking a banned substance (after Ernst Jean-Joseph of Haiti in 1974).

The match with Iran, who had lost 3-0 to Holland, was fast approaching. Scotland's preparation for that game had been less than ideal. 'We have to treat the next two matches like Bannockburn, for nothing less than victory over Iran and Holland will do,' said MacLeod at the Sierras Hotel. Andy Roxburgh, Scotland's Director of Coaching, had been at the match between Holland and Iran and gave MacLeod a report on what to expect.

Rioch and Masson had both struggled to impose themselves on the Peru game. Now Rioch was injured and could not play against Iran and Masson was dropped from the team. As in the Peru game, the Scots were all in blue to prevent a colour clash. Ali Parvin, the Iran midfielder, said: 'We will not be beaten easily by anyone. We have some very good players and Scotland will be surprised by the calibre of our play. If they underestimate us they will be in trouble.'

The locals' lack of interest in the match reflected Scotland's plummeting status. Only 10,000 turned up for the match in Cordoba. From the start, Iran's obvious strategy was to pack their penalty area with eight men at a time. After four minutes, John Robertson's corner was moved on by Macari towards goal but the ball was blocked. Jordan had also been presented with a half-chance before that but Scotland failed to build on those efforts and after 12 minutes Iran struck back. Jardine was caught out of position and Djahani put the ball into Faraki's path. He beat Rough but Jardine managed to make up enough ground to clear the ball as it edged towards the Scottish goal.

A free-kick from winger John Robertson, making his third Scotland appearance, produced an outstanding save from Hejazi, as did Dalglish's angled header. After half an hour, Buchan gave away a free-kick just outside the Scottish penalty area. Parvin took it and sent the ball only narrowly over the bar. Two minutes from half-time, Burns cut an incisive pass into the Iran penalty area. It caused confusion at the heart of the Iran defence as Jordan, goalkeeper Hejazi and centre-back Eskandarian all went for the ball. Hejazi and Jordan fell to the ground. Eskandarian was left to clear with no Scotland player near him. Unbelievably, he skewered the ball into his own net. Jordan and Dalglish looked almost sheepish as they acknowledged the goal.

Jordan, three minutes after half-time, tumbled in the box but referee Youssou N'Diaye of Senegal was uninterested in claims for a penalty. Five minutes later, Donachie accidentally kicked Buchan in the head. He had to be replaced by Forsyth. Immediately Forsyth and Burns got in a fankle and Faraki came close to an equalizer. On the hour, centre-forward Danaifar controlled the ball on the left wing, ducked past Archie Gemmill and trundled a shot between Rough and his near post for an equalizer. The defending of Gemmill and Jardine in the build-up to the goal had been less than convincing.

Scotland had never looked so impotent and Iran were not prepared to settle for a limited amount of glory. Outside-right Ghasem Pour broke quickly and Rough had to be sure of getting to the ball as he dived at the Iranian's feet to save. Dalglish, 15 minutes from time, found an opening but he shot softly into Hejazi's arms. It ended 1-1.

The fans jeered the team from the pitch and hurled their scarves at MacLeod and the Scotland players. The manager tried to put his feelings into words: 'I'm very sorry for the players but not so much for myself. They tried as hard as they could but never got a turn. We have to beat Holland 3-0 on Sunday and that doesn't look likely. The teamwork has gone wrong. Some of that has happened because of a loss of confidence. The players were under tremendous pressure today.' Gemmill, captain in place of Rioch, explained: 'The people to blame are the players, who did not play up to standard. If 11 players do not play to form then you never get anything. And we did not play to form. The manager and coach were not to blame. The players take the blame.'

Holland and Peru, meanwhile, had played out a 0-0 draw that was convenient to both of them.

Rioch said of MacLeod: 'I feel he has done the best in the circumstances. We are behind him. You can be assured whoever he picks for the Holland game will put everything into it. I am certain that the Dutch will have everyone in midfield bar two players up front. They will try to beat us there and if we lose a goal by trying to go forward then it's all over. It is a very bad position. We have to press on, looking for goals and keep things tight at the back for their breaks. And they will break better than the Peruvians.'

Happel stated that he would be happy to lose as long as it was not by more than three goals. Presuming that Peru beat Iran that would give the Dutch second place in the group and would also grant Happel's wish of avoiding the Brazilians in the next group phase. 'I doubt if even your fighting spirit can rise high enough now to give us any serious problems,' he said of the Scots.

MacLeod's confidence was restored as the game drew nearer: 'They are as good a squad as I could have wanted. All they have to do is show their average club form and we might be able to pull it off against Holland. We have at least 17 really great players in the squad and they always will be in my book, no matter what happens on Sunday.

(right) Tom Forsyth, a central defender, adds his weight to the Scottish cause as Scotland stretch Holland to the limit in their final group match in Mendoza, Argentina.

(below) A Scottish fan entertains the Argentinian crowd at the match between Scotland and Holland.

Nothing is insurmountable.'

A crowd of 40,000 were in Mendoza to see a fine match. There was a tangible sense of purpose about the Scots as they set about the business of the day. In action, it was expressed most clearly when, early on, Souness's cross was headed forcefully by Rioch against the bar with Dutch goalkeeper Jongbloed beaten. Hartford had two early shots; one was saved by Jongbloed, the other went screeching past a post.

Forsyth broke through the middle and put the ball in the net but offside was given against him. In the 10th minute Rioch collided with Neeskens, the key man for the Dutch. The encounter resulted in the Dutchman being taken to hospital.

Dalglish also had the ball in the net but the referee ruled it out for a foul by Jordan on a defender. Dalglish shot narrowly past, then Rough raced out of his penalty area to stop Rensenbrink progressing. In doing so he used his hands and a free-kick was awarded against him. It was luckily, not yet an automatic sending-off offence.

Ten minutes from half-time, Kennedy lost possession inside the Scottish half. Rep took the ball on and when the Dutch forward fell under the challenge of Rough and Kennedy inside the penalty area, referee Linemayr of Austria awarded a penalty. Gemmill was booked for protesting about the decision. Rob Rensenbrink sent it low to Alan Rough's right for the 1,000th goal of the World Cup finals.

A minute from half-time, Souness sent a long, diagonal pass to Jordan inside the Dutch penalty area. He headed the ball down to Dalglish who, eight yards from goal, whirled speedily to volley the ball high into the Dutch net for an excellent equalizing goal.

Joe Jordan puts the Dutch defence under pressure.

Kenny Dalglish volleys Scotland's equalizer against Holland.

Archie Gemmill successfully guides the ball through the Dutch defence as Scotland seek their third goal.

With the Dutch defence in his wake, Gemmill has now made some space for himself inside their penalty area but he is confronted by Jongbloed, the Dutch goal-keeper.

A minute the other side of half-time, Souness was again at the heart of the action. Dalglish's cross and Rioch's header sent him on a run into the Dutch penalty area that was ended when Rensenbrink brought him down. Linemayr again awarded a penalty and Gemmill sent it inside Jongbloed's left-hand post. Now there was some hope.

Scotland continued to press and, on 68 minutes, Dalglish moved dangerously towards the Dutch goal. When he was tackled by Krol the ball broke to Gemmill. The midfielder veered round Jansen, steered the ball under the two-footed lunge of Poortvliet, and put the ball through Krol's legs before curling it, left-footed, over the advancing Jongbloed. It was the individual goal of the 1978 World Cup and it got the Argentinian crowd to their feet as Gemmill jogged away, fist clenched in gritty defiance. Scotland now needed just one more goal.

Three minutes later, Rep exchanged passes with Krol in midfield, advanced a few steps and directed a 30-yard shot high into the Scottish net for the third outstanding goal of an outstanding game. It was the end of the scoring. Scotland won, 3-2, but lost their fight to stay in the World Cup.

MacLeod said afterwards: 'The players and myself decided before the match to say, "To hell with everyone" and play as we can play. I would like to say that this has been a very disciplined squad, both on and off the field. Tonight the squad simply said, "Stuff the lot of them". And we showed just how well we can play.' Rioch added: 'We knew before the game against Holland that it was difficult to qualify. We had a short talk and then decided to go out and play our own way.'

Happel said: 'I was not surprised at seeing Scotland play so well. It was just a surprise to me that they had not done so earlier. They were ahead of us tonight in everything. I was disappointed with my team's performance.'

'I'll come back from Argentina either a millionaire or a condemned man,' MacLeod had said before the World Cup. The unexpectedness of the victory over the Dutch and the narrowness, after everything, of the Scots' failure to qualify, again on goal difference, had restored his standing to some extent but he was still not expected to survive as manager. On 17 June, Tom Lauchlan, chairman of the SFA's International Committee, said: 'I thought Ally MacLeod was a good choice when he was appointed. I still think that. I've no reservations about saying MacLeod should not be made a scapegoat.' MacLeod would stay on.

He still came in for a great deal of retrospective criticism. Much was made of him not going to see Peru or Iran before the World Cup. Yet the Peruvian manager had not seen Scotland play. And against the Dutch, the Scots' most successful game, the key to

Gemmill, with maximum precision, swerves the ball over Jongbloed as the goal-keeper dives at his feet.

The job done, Gemmill raises his fist in celebration as the Argentinian fans rise from their seats in acclaim of his artistry. Gemmill had just scored the most exceptional goal of the 1978 tournament.

their victory had not been a detailed knowledge of the opposition but a determination to play to the Scots' own strengths. Watching opponents is of little worth unless your own players perform at their best – that had not happened in either of the first two games. Back in 1973, at the start of the Scots' run of 1970s success, Willie Ormond had dismissed the idea of worrying about the opposition – in that case a Czech side better then Iran or Peru.

Sightings of drunken Scottish players were like UFOs – lots of detailed descriptions but no pictures in evidence

MacLeod's training routines were criticized but the Dutch had hardly bothered training at all. Had MacLeod followed that policy he would have received even more flak. There were reports of angry disputes between the players and the SFA over financial matters, with MacLeod caught in the middle. The Dutch, however, had spent the year leading up to the World Cup haggling over cash with their FA.

Happel constantly argued with his players ... all the way to the final, proof that the important thing was how players performed on the pitch when it mattered. Scotland's victory, after all, in their final game, hadn't come about through extensive reconstruction of the side. There were only three changes in the team for the Holland game from the one that had faced Peru in the opening match. Their approach and their attitude, however, was different. They had also been unlucky to lose McGrain – a genuine world-class performer – and McQueen, a highly effective and greatly underrated centre-back, from their defence. Both of those players had played vital roles in the qualification stages. They could not be replaced in time for the finals.

Nebulous stories of wild drinking, gambling and womanizing among the Scottish players, were press inventions. Unfortunately, they were made believable by the Scots' distracted-looking performances in their first two matches and were spread by those who took great delight in tales of Scottish partying. One of the rumours was of the Scots' liking for whisky. 'They smoke and drink a lot – all sorts of alcohol, especially whisky,' said a Tunisian official, probably not too familiar with alcohol. This sounded more like an image conjured up from *Whisky Galore* than the young Scottish footballers of the 1970s. For all these tales, there were few reliable, credible accounts of such behaviour or pictures of it. Sightings of drunken Scottish players were like UFOs – lots of detailed descriptions but no pictures in evidence.

MacLeod was panned by the press – after the event – for saying that Scotland would win the World Cup. However, Matt Busby, one of the greatest-ever Scottish managers, had said the same thing in the 1950s. Willie Ormond and his captain Billy Bremner had repeatedly said the same thing in 1974 while in 1978 Don Masson, Bruce Rioch and others had voiced this belief. And the series of results and performances between MacLeod's taking over in May 1977 and the World Cup in June 1978 did give grounds for optimism. It was only after the 1978 tournament that it became clear to all Scots just how difficult it was to get close to winning the World Cup.

MacLeod's infectious, extrovert nature made him the natural focus of a personality cult that grew outrageously in fanaticism. Press and public went along with it unquestioningly; only the truly phlegmatic remained unaffected. Journalists and fans had caught the mood. Now, blinded by the hangover from the party, they were smarting. MacLeod had been made the whipping boy for a nation that had forgotten the usual checks and balances when assessing any issue and who had come to believe their own 'Wha's like us?' publicity. When combined with the Scots' undying fanaticism for football it made for an explosive blend. Attacking Ally MacLeod was easier than Scots taking a long, hard look at themselves.

A GOAL FIESTA

SPAIN, 1982

The unexpected, exhilarating pleasure of leading Brazil lasted just a quarter of an hour.

On 20 September 1978, Scotland played their first match after the World Cup in Argentina, away to Austria in Vienna. Alan Rough struggled for form and Joe Jordan and Andy Gray appeared incompatible as a striking partnership. The team was, however, unlucky to lose 3-2 to Austria in a European Championship match in the Prater Stadium. Six days later, Ally MacLeod quit the Scotland manager's job to return to Ayr United, where he had begun his managerial career in 1967. 'I just feel that now is the proper time to go,' he said. 'I've never regretted being the national manager. It was my ambition to have the job and I've done it. I would like to think that I achieved something by helping to take Scotland to the World Cup.'

Jock Stein, meanwhile, had parted company with Celtic in May 1978. Stein had then become manager of Leeds United and, at the time of MacLeod's resignation, was on the verge of signing a contract with Leeds worth £30,000 a year. On 2 October, a meeting of the SFA's International Committee decided to make an approach to Stein to ask him to become manager of Scotland. Stein's wife's was deeply attached to Scotland and not keen on moving to England. Her feelings influenced his thinking as he weighed up the two job offers and on 4 October, two days before his 56th birthday, Stein became Scotland manager with a four-year contract worth £100,000.

He had already proved himself the most accomplished manager in Scottish football history. In 13 years at Celtic he had made them one of the most respected names in European football. He had spent a modicum of money in winning 25 trophies with the club, including nine championships in succession. The peak of his career had been the winning of the European Cup in 1967. Every member of that side had been Scots-born and it had been mooted at the time that the Scottish national team should simply be the Celtic team in dark blue jerseys. For political reasons, however, that had never been likely to happen.

In 1977, Stein had won the double of Scottish Cup and League for the sixth time but in the summer of that year, team captain Kenny Dalglish had left for Liverpool. Celtic's other key player, Danny McGrain, had suffered an ankle injury that kept him out of the Celtic team for most of that season. Even Stein's managerial powers could not rescue that situation and Celtic had suffered a poor season. Stein's replacement by Billy McNeill in May 1978 left the way open for the fresh challenge of managing the national team. He had been there before, on a part-time basis, for World Cup qualifying matches against Finland, Italy and Poland in 1965, and had almost succeeded in taking Scotland to the 1966 finals.

'Promises are easy to make but very difficult to keep,' said Stein. 'Scotland's success has to be won on the park and this will be the job of players. I will ask the fans to back me; but only if they think I'm worth it.' The first two years of Stein's manager

> *'Promises are easy to make but very difficult to keep,' said Jock Stein. 'Scotland's success has to be won on the park'*

Joe Jordan opens the scoring against Sweden at Hampden.

ship were taken up with European Championship qualifiers. The Scots' group was won by Belgium, eventual runners-up in the 1980 finals in Italy. By the time of Scotland's World Cup qualifier with Sweden in Stockholm in September 1980, it was very much Stein's team that took the field: Rough, McGrain, F. Gray, Miller, McLeish, Hansen, Dalglish, Sturrock, A. Gray, Gemmill, Robertson. It was an attacking formation. Full-backs Frank Gray and Danny McGrain were speedy overlappers while Alan Hansen, a centre-back, was at his best when bringing the ball out of defence.

The game was evenly matched throughout the first half with both Scotland and Sweden making and missing chances. With 17 minutes of the match remaining, Gordon Strachan found midfield partner Archie Gemmill and drove on to take the return in his stride. Strachan then sent a scoring shot from left to right across goalkeeper Hellstrom. It was a piece of no-nonsense precision, beautifully symbolic of a new geometrically methodical, calculating Scottish side; Stein had constructed his team around the Aberdeen, Liverpool and Nottingham Forest clubs who won consistently in Europe using such methods.

In their other opening matches in the group, Scotland achieved two dour draws with Portugal and Northern Ireland at Hampden – watched by a combined attendance of 140,000 – and home and away wins over Israel. Stein favoured no particular players and showed no unbending loyalty to anyone.

A year after the meeting with Sweden at the Solna Stadium, the Scandinavians were at Hampden for the return. 'Oh Flower of Norway', sang the Scots fans in the queue snaking its way into Glasgow's Central Station on hearing that, earlier in the day, England had lost their World Cup qualifier in Oslo. They were among 81,511 who travelled to Hampden, paying £2–£2.50 for terracing tickets and £5–£7 for the stand.

Sweden had remade their team after the defeat by Scotland and they now had a revived chance of taking one of the two qualifying positions. 'All through my career as a manager I have preferred to play against sides with something to play for,' said Stein. 'That way you are always on your toes.' Stein had promised an attacking performance, and in the first minute Dalglish's shot on the turn forced Ravelli into a diving save. Ten minutes later, Dalglish's perceptive pass was taken on by Hartford. He had the ball in the net and appeared unlucky to be given offside. A Wark header went narrowly wide as the Scots proved inspired by another great Hampden occasion. The Scots were moving the ball about at incredible speed and were showing exquisite passing skills.

Ravelli failed to cut out a cross from Davie Provan and Dalglish looked certain to score but he fluffed his header and the Swedes cleared. It had been the best scoring chance up until then. After 20 minutes, Robertson was fouled as he moved down the left wing. His free-kick went towards Jordan who once again provided the cue for a Hampden crowd to burst into September song. His header rushed past Ravelli, nicked the underside of the crossbar and sped into the Swedish net.

A goal-line clearance by McGrain soon after half-time and a magnificent save by Rough maintained Scotland's lead. They then went back on the attack but, with ten minutes remaining, had failed to get the goal they needed. Jordan was put clear on Ravelli but he nipped his shot over the bar. A minute later, Andy Gray, who had replaced Dalglish, found himself in possession inside the penalty area. Moving away from goal and looking of little threat to the Swedes, he brushed against a defender, threw out his arms and hit the turf. Swiss referee Andre Daina gave the desired penalty. John Robertson stepped up and, with his easy action, sent the ball past Ravelli. Gray, to Stein's chagrin, later said it had not been a penalty.

Scotland now needed just one point from their final two games, in Belfast and in Lisbon, to qualify for the World Cup finals in Spain. A desultory draw against Northern Ireland that October saw them achieve their goal. The Irish finished in second place in the group and would also be in Madrid in January for the draw for the finals. It was rumoured before the draw took place that Scotland would be based in Malaga and in the same group as Brazil. That was how the 'draw' turned out. Initially, however, the Scots had been placed in the same group as Argentina. Then it was announced that an error had been made. Also in Scotland's group were New Zealand and the USSR. The Scots would stay at the Campo de Golf, Sotogrande, so there would be many opportunities for SFA officials, large numbers of whom now attended World Cups with the official party, to get to work on their handicaps. For the players, however, it meant a hellish journey to and from matches along Spain's southern coastal road.

The Brazilians would, again, be indulging in three months of World Cup preparation. The Soviets spent three weeks in southern Spain in January, then a fortnight there in February. It was a depth of preparation that Scotland could not match; club football still retained priority over the international game. The Scots were also in Spain in February, losing a friendly with the hosts 3-0. Before flying to Valencia to play that match, they had recorded their World Cup song, 'We Have a Dream'. It was a reflective ballad, featuring actor John Gordon Sinclair on vocals, with the non-specific ambition of wishing to 'score the winning goal' for 'Bonnie Scotland'. Ambitions had been modified since Argentina. The record reached Number 5 in the British charts.

Stein had been unhappy with some of the defensive mistakes made in that game with Spain. For another friendly, against Holland in March, Allan Evans, the Aston Villa centre-back, won his first cap, as did Jim Bett, a midfielder with Rangers. David Narey, the Dundee United defender, made his first Scotland appearance of that season. Complacency was unlikely to set in while Stein was around. 'The more people challenging the better and I want the men who play tomorrow night to justify their selection and put the pressure on others. At this stage, players should be hoping and working to go to Spain, not expecting to do so. For the World Cup finals you really need two different sides. What will do in one game won't necessarily do in another. That's why this game is so important.'

There were 72,000 at Hampden to see a 2-1 win over Holland, achieved through goals from Frank Gray and Dalglish. Evans and Bett were particularly impressive. Dalglish's goal was a classic. Jordan sent him clear with a sweet back-heel, Dalglish swept away from the Dutch defence and as goalkeeper Van Breukelen came towards him he pitched the ball over the hefty Dutchman. Now 31, Dalglish was using all his experience to better his own high standards.

In early April, Argentinian troops invaded and occupied the Falkland Islands, British territories in the South Atlantic. Britain responded by sending troops to retake the islands. There were suggestions that the three British qualifiers – Scotland, Northern Ireland and England – might have to pull out if the conflict continued into

June, when the World Cup began. Graeme Souness and Danny McGrain had said that they believed Scotland should withdraw if the fighting was still taking place. Kenny Dalglish was of the opinion that, as Argentina was the aggressor, FIFA should ask them to withdraw from the World Cup. (Had FIFA done so, public pressure in Argentina might well have ended the Falklands crisis immediately).

In April, Scotland started the Home Internationals with a 1-1 draw in Belfast. They defeated Wales 1-0 at Hampden in May but in the 100th Scotland v England game on 29 May, Scotland were listless in a 1-0 defeat; Rough was overpowered by Mariner as the striker scored England's goal. By then, McGrain and Souness had taken account of public opinion on the World Cup/Falkland Islands situation. Many members of the British task forces wanted the team to participate in the World Cup; good performances might even help the troops' morale. That being so, said the players, they now saw no dilemma in going to the World Cup.

On 4 June, the Scotland squad flew to the Algarve for World Cup preparation. There they warmed up with wins on successive evenings in bounce games against the Portuguese Third Division side Torralto by 9-1 and 7-0. Scotland moved on to Spain on 11 June. Johan Cruyff, who had commentated on the Scotland v Holland friendly, tipped Scotland as the most likely of the outsiders to go far at the Spanish World Cup.

New Zealand, their first opponents, had played 15 matches to get to the World Cup and in beating Fiji 13-0 set a World Cup scoring record. They were managed by John Adshead, a Lancastrian, and their squad included several English and Scottish players who had played low-grade professional football in Britain and now had New Zealand nationality.

In the 1981–82 season, the SFA had made the decision to adopt 'Scotland the Brave' as the Scots' new pre-match anthem, as opposed to 'God Save the Queen'. Before the New Zealand game, a wonky representation of this tune blared out unsteadily from the stadium's public address system. It was less than inspiring.

'Against Brazil, we want at least a draw or, if possible, a win. But I am prepared to sacrifice going all out for a victory,' said Stein

Stein said: 'I have chosen as many proven goalscorers as possible without leaving the way open for them to run through us at the back. But the main thing is for us to win whether it be by one, two or more goals. Two points in the opening match would mean that when we play Russia in our final group game we have a live situation.' New Zealand fielded three Scots-born players: Sam Malcolmson, their centre-back, who had once played for Albion Rovers, Allan Boath and Adrian Elrick. On 15 June, the day Scotland faced New Zealand, Argentina finally surrendered the Falkland Islands to Britain.

New Zealand's initial aim was to prevent Scotland scoring in the opening 20 minutes. They were within two minutes of attaining that objective when Strachan swayed past three New Zealanders and slipped the ball to Kenny Dalglish who clipped it past New Zealand goalkeeper Van Hattum. On the half hour, Strachan passed to Ally Brazil. Van Hattum parried the striker's shot and Wark swept the rebound into the New Zealand net. Two minutes later, Strachan picked out Wark with a cross and the midfielder put a powerful header past Van Hattum. New Zealand appeared to have nothing to offer as an attacking force and there was no further scoring by half-time. The 15,000 Scottish fans in the 20,000 crowd at La Rosaleda stadium were in relaxed mood as they awaited the second half.

More goals for Scotland appeared to be a formality. Soon after the restart, Dalglish twisted past a New Zealand defender and put the ball in Brazil's path directly in front of goal. His shot went wildly over the bar. Brazil was swiftly replaced by Archibald, another striker who rarely repeated his club form at international level. Another goal followed a minute later. Rufer outpaced the slow-looking Gray and crossed. The ball was intercepted by McGrain who played it towards Rough but did not put enough weight on his pass. Sumner darted in between the two Scots and hit a shot that Rough half-blocked. Sumner put the loose ball in the net. The Kiwis, encouraged by this,

THE SCOTTISH WORLD CUP SQUAD
We Have a Dream

OFFICIAL SCOTTISH WORLD CUP SQUAD SINGLE
Photograph by courtesy of THE SCOTTISH DAILY RECORD

Jock Stein hovers outside the Scottish dugout during the bittersweet 5-2 win over New Zealand that opened the action for Scotland at the 1982 finals.

exerted more pressure. On 65 minutes, a ball played from midway inside the New Zealand half put Woodin in behind the Scottish defence. Again, Rough was beaten.

With a quarter of an hour remaining, Souness and Gray stood behind the ball at a Scottish free-kick. They appeared to dither over what to do, then John Robertson stepped up to scoop a beautifully judged chip over the New Zealand defensive wall and high into their net. Dalglish forced Van Hattum into a good save before Scotland got a fifth with 10 minutes to go. Strachan's corner found Archibald and he bent a header past Van Hattum.

Over the following few days, the Spanish waiters on the Costa Del Sol, serving beer in gigantic glasses, would be raving about Strachan's performance. The midfielder had been at his best but Stein, in common with most Scots, had mixed feelings about the overall performance of the team: 'We are still the greatest nation for punishing ourselves at every turn. New Zealand should be proud of their performance but I think we did assist them. We had one or two self-inflicted wounds. They scored twice with two very bad goals to give away at international level.'

Scotland were top of their group after the win over New Zealand but they now faced an entirely different challenge – Brazil in Seville's magnificent Benito Villamarin stadium. 'We could win in Seville and still go out if we lose next Tuesday. That's why the Russian game is the key to it all and I can't afford to go knocking hell out of the players before that. It may sound as if I'm dismissing the Brazil game but that's not so. Although they have always been my favourites to win the World Cup I think we can do well against them. We want at least a draw or, if possible, a win but I am prepared to sacrifice going all out for victory. We simply must keep something in the bank for Tuesday,' said Stein.

Brazil were in their 12th consecutive World Cup finals and their manager Tele Santana had been dismissive of Scotland before the tournament, saying they were a typically hard-running British side who were limited technically. The previous Monday, his team had beaten the USSR 2-1 in a superb match.

The day of the match against Brazil, the temperature in Seville was close to 100 degrees until long after dusk. The match began at 9 p.m. Spanish time, and in the 47,000 crowd there were 20,000 Scots fans, happily rubbing shoulders with 6,000 Brazilians. The main surprise in the Scottish team was the omission of Dalglish;

perhaps, as he had hinted, Stein was saving him for the match with the USSR. Dalglish was on the substitutes' bench.

After 18 minutes, Souness hooked a long, high ball to the right. Wark climbed to head it down forcefully. It sat up perfectly for Narey, close to the edge of the Brazilian 18-yard box. Archibald's decoy run created some space for Narey but three Brazilian defenders gathered round him. On the move, he quickly controlled the ball with his left instep, then made the perfect connection with his right foot to crack it high into the Brazilian net. It was one of the finest goals of that World Cup, one to match the best the Brazilians could concoct. It was all the more astonishing for being scored by a full-back – Narey looked more surprised than anyone as he danced with delight. High on the terraces behind the goal into which Narey had scored, Spanish fans passed wine-filled goatskins to Scotland's followers in recognition of a fine contribution to the ongoing spectacle.

The unexpected, exhilarating pleasure of leading Brazil lasted just a quarter of an hour. Hansen fouled Cerezo and Zico's 25-yard free-kick drifted high past the static Rough to make it 1-1. Two minutes later, a cross from Eder deceived Rough, leaving Brazilian striker Serginho poised to head his side into the lead. Instead, he topped it, putting his header over the bar.

(top)
David Narey moves quickly to shoot at goal as Brazilian defenders converge on him in Seville.

(centre)
Having made a clean connection, Narey watches as the ball streaks towards the Brazilian goal.

(bottom)
Narey leaps with joy as he begins the celebrations for the goal of his life.

Five minutes after half-time, a Socrates shot was deflected behind by Hansen. Junior took the corner and Oscar met the ball at the near post to head Brazil's second goal. Souness had been marking him but his challenge for the ball looked more like a training-game effort than one suitable for a match in the World Cup finals. Midway through the half, Wark got on the end of a Hartford cross. He could have headed for goal but tried instead to lay it back. The Brazilians cleared before any Scots could challenge for the ball.

Brazil were passing the ball around in stunning style. Socrates found Serginho in the midfield and his turn and pass opened up an enormous gap between Eder and the Scottish defence. He advanced into the Scottish penalty area to put Brazil further ahead with a chip from 15 yards. After that, Robertson went close for Scotland, shooting narrowly over the bar. In the 86th minute, another rapid Brazilian move ended with Falcão, 20 yards out, swiftly drawing back his right foot to shoot and score Brazil's fourth goal.

Stein commented: 'It is never easy to accept defeat but against a team like Brazil it is no disgrace. Brazil showed tonight that they are good enough to win the World Cup. Until half-time we had as much of the game but after losing that early second-half goal we were always chasing the game. We faced the same problem as Russia in that we are unaccustomed to playing in conditions like this.' Tele Santana said he felt sorry for Scotland but that he believed they would now miss out on qualification for the second stage. 'We were very concerned in the first half because the Scots played well and caused us problems. But Zico's goal was the turning point for us.'

A host of fire engines and ambulances had stood by outside the stadium in case of emergency. As the Scottish and Brazilian fans ambled back into the city centre down a wide avenue late that Friday night, they were treated to the sight of Scottish fans, kilted-out in full regalia, hitching a lift on the back of a fire engine. It had been a special night, with the colour, action and music on the terraces rivalling the proceedings on the field.

The evening after Scotland's defeat by Brazil, the USSR defeated New Zealand 3-0. The Soviets now had a better goal difference than Scotland and needed only a draw from the match between the two to qualify. Scotland were third in their group on goal difference. Stein said: 'We have to go out and win the match and that suits our natural style. If we had only to draw we could have gone out with a defensive set-up and tossed it away, because history proves that nobody beats us better than ourselves. Now we must go and put pressure on them. Although they're obviously the favourites, we have a lot going for us. Apart from Brazil, I haven't seen any other side in this tour-

Oscar of Brazil wins the ball in the air from Scotland's Steve Archibald.

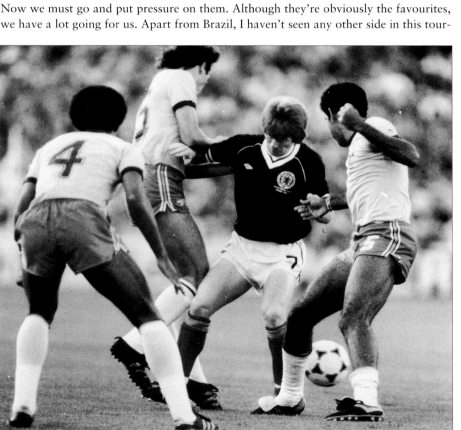

Gordon Strachan, Scotland's most creative individual of the 1982 World Cup, is manoevred off the ball by Brazilian defenders.

nament play as well as we did in the first 45 minutes on Friday. There hasn't been a team more aggressive than us and only ourselves and Hungary were not afraid of our opening games.

'It is never easy to accept defeat but against a team like Brazil it is no disgrace'

'We're very proud of our supporters. They do help us but I've never seen a fan score a goal. On Tuesday night our main fans will be the players who wear the dark blue jerseys. A goal in the first minute is no more valuable than a goal in the final minute, provided it's the only one of the game. Of course we would love that kind of a start but it is more important that we give a controlled performance. Of course we must take the initiative but we must be sensible about it. Can we afford to gamble everything on, say, 20 minutes of all-out aggression? I don't think so, for it could all be thrown away with those tactics.'

Stein's disregard for reputations was shown clearly before the match: in Malaga, Kenny Dalglish would watch the game from the stand, among the 35,000 crowd. The unexpected replacement for Dalglish was Joe Jordan, now 31, who had struggled for fitness after being injured prior to the World Cup. It appeared a massive gamble by Stein but the striker would not let him down. The Soviets, expecting to face Dalglish's subtle skills, found it difficult to cope with Jordan's more openly aggressive style. After sitting out the first two games he unleashed enormous energy on this one. After ten minutes, Robertson crossed and Jordan met the ball with a diving header. The ball went flying goalwards but Dasaev, the USSR goalkeeper, prodded it past his post.

Rough grasped the ball at Blokhin's feet as the Soviets countered. Then, on 15 minutes, Jordan again showed his all-out commitment in the finest fashion. Narey's huge punt from defence was cut out by Chivadze but he couldn't control the ball, which was intercepted by Archibald. He pushed it into Jordan's path and, showing magnificent composure, the striker placed the ball past Dasaev and into the net.

Ten minutes later, Baltacha appeared to handle inside his penalty area. The Romanian referee Nicolae Rainea awarded a corner from which Jordan's header missed the target. Scotland were playing controlled football but it was driven by pure passion. They reached half-time with their lead intact and, shortly after the restart, first Archibald, then Wark, then Robertson almost added to the lead. Jordan continued

Joe Jordan (left) is congratulated by Frank Gray after his opening goal against the Soviet Union. Jordan had trained like a demon to be fit for the World Cup after sustaining a serious knee injury while playing for Milan. Jordan played every game as if it was his last and this match, which did turn out to be his last for his country, was a personal triumph for him He went out in some style.

giving his all – one cameo, when he challenged a Soviet defender, was priceless. As the ball rolled towards the goal-line, Scottish fans were presented with the awesome sight of Jordan shoulder-to-shoulder with his marker, his face a mask of intense determination and effort. It was a sight to inspire the most casual Scotland fan – not that were many of those about!

On the hour, some swift Soviet interpassing ended with a shot from Gavrilov that went spinning wildly after being blocked by Narey. It fell to Chivadze who swept the ball over Rough for the USSR's equalizer. With 13 minutes remaining, Demianenko pushed Wark inside the penalty area but again Rainea was unwilling to award a penalty against his Soviet comrades. The Scots continued to bring the best out in

Dasaev but five minutes from time, Hansen and Miller made the basic mistake of both going for the same ball. They collided and the ball fell to Shengalia. He sprinted away with only Rough to beat. It took only a dip of the shoulder from Shengalia for the goalkeeper to buy his dummy and dive in the wrong direction. The USSR man duly delivered the ball into the unguarded goal.

With four minutes remaining, Robertson gave Souness possession of the ball just outside the USSR penalty area and the Scottish captain held on to the ball under pressure before hitting a low shot that touched the inside of the post on its way into the net. The score remained 2-2 at the final whistle. For the third successive World Cup, Scotland were out on goal difference. Stein said afterwards: 'I am very disappointed we have not qualified. If we had played the way we did in any other section we would have gone through. We are quite proud of the side, of their attitude and tactical application. I think once again we were on the wrong end of a vital decision. The players assure me that John Wark was pushed inside the box. It was definitely a penalty. We have proved we can compete at this level, if not win. After all, there are only two or three teams who can come here to the finals expecting to take the trophy. Tonight I think we have done Scotland proud, on and off the field.

'The talk about Scotland winning the World Cup isn't even imaginable. I suppose it's the stuff that dreams are made of for a nation of our size but we all came over here full of enthusiasm and hopes that we would do well and we almost made it. I know we're always sorry for ourselves but on this occasion I think we're entitled to feel that way. There are teams still in this competition who don't have 50 per cent of our ability.'

Stein had been the first Scotland manager to fully use a squad system over three World Cup finals matches. 'Not too many managers survive World Cups. It's a miracle if you do,' he said. There were, however, not too many managers like him.

Graeme Souness, the Scotland captain, finds a narrow opening in the Soviet Union defence to score Scotland's last-gasp goal in the 2-2 draw in Malaga.

Muted celebrations follow Graeme Souness' equalizer against the Soviet Union. The goal meant that for the third consecutive World Cup Scotland went out of the tournament on goal difference.

HOT COMPETITION

MEXICO, 1986

'There is nothing between all four sides and luck will play a big part in deciding who finishes in the first two in our group.'

Franz Beckenbauer after watching Scotland's 3–0 victory over Romania

Kenny Dalglish, after being dropped for the match with the USSR in Malaga, had seemed to have a precarious future as a Scotland player. The next two years had, however, seen some of his best-ever Scotland performances even though the Scots had again been pipped by Belgium for a place in the 1984 European Championship finals. As Scotland approached the qualifiers for the 1986 World Cup, they relied on Dalglish more than ever.

The key game for Scotland arrived early. After a 3-0 home win over Iceland in their first qualifier, they faced Spain – finalists in the European Championships the previous summer – at Hampden on 14 November 1984.

Miguel Muñoz, the Spain manager, had coached Real Madrid to their 7-3 win over Eintracht Frankfurt in the European Cup final at Hampden in 1960. He said on his arrival in Glasgow: 'We are not here for a 0-0 draw. Spain want to win at a ground I know so well.'

Kenny Dalglish battles his way through the Spanish defence in the World Cup in the qualifier at Hampden in November 1984. Thirteen years after his Scotland début, Dalglish's contribution to the national team was greater than ever.

Jock Stein had carried out extensive reconstruction to his side since the World Cup of 1982, but though Dalglish had had a knee injury when the squad for the Spain match was chosen, he was still one of the names picked by the manager. The Scottish team to play Spain was: Leighton, Nicol, Albiston, McLeish, Miller, McStay, Souness, Bett, Dalglish, Johnston, Cooper. For the first time since Stein had taken over in 1978, he was able to name an unchanged team from the previous match. 'Spain know we will be coming at them,' said Stein. 'But we will have to chase them sensibly. There is more pressure on Spain than on us. They are European Championship finalists, but they won't worry about proving their class. Their one concern is getting a result.'

Some terracing tickets at £3 were still on sale on the day of the game and the eventual crowd of 74,299 saw a game few would forget. Jim Bett and Davie Cooper both hit a Spanish post in the opening half-hour. In the 32nd minute, Scotland were awarded a corner, which Dalglish took. McLeish headed the ball goalwards but it was blocked and reached Nicol, whose shot was half-stopped by Spanish goalkeeper Arconada. The ball bounced up off the surface and striker Mo Johnston dived to head it into the net. Ten minutes later, Bett sent a cross to the back post. Johnston climbed above two Spanish defenders to direct a header past Arconada. Scotland relaxed slightly after that and midway through the second half Spain got a freak goal. Comacho's free-kick reached centre-back Goicoechea, who headed downwards. As Jim Leighton, the Scottish goalkeeper, dived, the ball bounced high over him and into the net.

With just over a quarter of an hour remaining, Cooper nudged the ball to Dalglish close to the Spanish goal-line and just inside their penalty area. Four Spanish defenders converged on him from various directions. With the ball on his left foot he made as if to shoot. The Spanish defenders paused slightly, waiting to see where the ball would go. That gave Dalglish the split-second he needed and he took the ball a few inches away from Maceda, who had been blocking Dalglish's sight of goal. Two more defenders stampeded in his direction but he now had the gap he needed and he flighted the ball between them with absolutely nothing to spare. It curled round Arconada and pelted against the back stanchion to seal Scotland's win.

Dalglish's goal was the best seen in a World Cup tie at Hampden and it matched the standard of the overall performance which, for quality, was on a par with the one against Czechoslovakia in 1977. It made for 30 goals in 96 internationals for Dalglish, an exceptional feat for a player who was as effective at making goals for others as he

Dalglish (right) is congratulated by Graeme Souness (left) and Alex McLeish (centre) after his stunning goal against Spain. Scotland fans on the Hampden terraces also show their approval.

was in scoring them himself.

Stein, talking about Dalglish afterwards, said: 'He could so easily have called off from this match. It was touch and go. He has done very little training since he joined us on Monday and has had ice pack treatment. Kenny's decision to play was one of the most courageous I've ever known in all my years as a manager. Kenny is something else. Even when he is being tackled hard he is so experienced that he anticipates the kicks and rides forward with them so that he isn't badly hurt.

'This is my most satisfying win since I became Scotland manager. The great thing is that they are all playing as a team. That really excites me.'

Muñoz said: 'The Scots were fantastic. It was the most powerful Scottish side I have ever seen. I was not disappointed with my team. We were simply beaten by a better side.'

Scotland now had a base to build on for the rest of the qualifying series. However, Dalglish was available for only one of their remaining four qualifying matches. He missed the return against Spain through injury and Scotland lost 1-0. He was back for the match with Wales at Hampden in March 1985 but this ended in a shocking 1-0 home defeat. In May, Dalglish was with Liverpool for their European Cup final as the Scots managed a 1-0 win in Iceland. And as the Scots approached their final qualifying match, in Wales, Dalglish had to miss out through having stitches in a leg wound. Graeme Souness was suspended and Johnston missed the match with a thigh strain. Both Alan Hansen and Steve Archibald were unavailable through injury.

Spain had recovered from their Hampden setback to take advantage of Scotland's string of poor results. Now, a win or a draw in Cardiff was essential for the Scots to finish second in their group and take the prize of a play-off for a place in the finals. The line-up was: Leighton, Gough, Malpas, Aitken, McLeish, Miller, Nicol, Strachan, Sharp, Bett, Speedie. It was a team built for battle. Stein, who intended to retire after the finals in Mexico, said beforehand: 'They'll compete all right, and that's something we didn't do when Wales beat us at Hampden but there is also a lot of skill in this side.'

After 13 minutes, Hughes, the Welsh striker, bustled through the Scottish defence

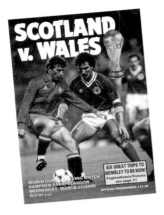

Jock Stein on the touchline at Ninian Park, Cardiff on the night of Scotland's World Cup qualifier with Wales in September 1985. The evening would end tragically with the sudden death of Stein.

to shoot Wales into the lead. The Scots responded with incessant pressure until the 81st minute when Speedie shot and David Phillips was struck on the hand by the ball. Davie Cooper, Rangers' skilful winger, took the responsibility of the penalty. A miss would almost certainly end Scotland's interest in that World Cup. The winger showed enormous composure to direct a low, left-footed shot past Southall's outstretched left-hand.

Scotland held on for the draw. There were thousands of Scots fans in Wales that night but none of them would be celebrating after the match. Football, which often uses heavy words lightly, was to experience a tragedy. Close to the end of the match Jock Stein collapsed in the dugout. He was carried to the Ninian Park medical room where he died.

Scotland's team doctor Stuart Hillis, a heart surgeon, said: 'At 9.15, Mr Stein collapsed and was taken to the medical room. On examining him he had a heart attack and required emergency treatment. There was a full resuscitation team there and the facilities were excellent but a cardiogram showed there was no heart function at that stage. After 30 minutes of every possible treatment the procedure was terminated. Death was evident at 9.50. I have been Mr Stein's consultant for more than a year and I was treating him for a condition unrelated to what happened tonight. He probably began to feel ill midway through the second half. There was no reason before the game to think there was something brewing. This was a sudden death that could have happened at any time.'

Ten thousand people lined the streets as Stein's funeral cortège made its way to the Linn Crematorium in Glasgow two days later. A wreath from the Scottish football squad read: 'We will miss you boss.' Scotland mourned – Stein's strength and dignity had exerted a marked effect on many people, both inside and outside football. He was entirely irreplaceable.

Alex Ferguson, manager of Aberdeen, had been assisting Stein with Scotland since 1984. He agreed to take over the team manager's duties. His first task would be to prepare the team for the play-off, on a home-and-away basis, with Australia, winners of the Oceania group.

Gordon Strachan on the ball against Australia in the first leg of the play-off for a place in the 1986 World Cup. The Australians had arrived in Glasgow with a reputation as a tough team who would make up in muscle what they lacked in skill. On the night, Scottish guile proved too much for the Australians to cope with.

The first leg was at Hampden in November 1985 and the Scottish strikeforce for the match had 100 caps between them. Dalglish was making his 99th appearance for Scotland; Frank McAvennie, who had been scoring ceaselessly for West Ham, his first. 'If we go to Melbourne with a two-goal lead I'll be happy,' said Ferguson. 'One goal would mean a helluva hard match down under.' Two goals in two minutes pleased him and the 62,000 who watched. The first was a crafty free-kick from Cooper, the second a smart pass from Dalglish finished by a touch over the goalkeeper's body by the outstanding McAvennie.

After a 30-hour trip, the squad arrived in Australia on 29 November, five days before the second leg of the play-off at the Olympic Park Stadium in Melbourne. Souness, now with Sampdoria, arrived from Italy at 5 a.m. the day before the game. It was shown live on Channel 4 from 9 a.m. Pubs all over Scotland were given special licences to open in the morning. In Melbourne, approximately half the 29,000 crowd were Scots. Several fine saves by Leighton gave Scotland a 0-0 draw in a match in which they had rarely looked like scoring. 'We defended well. We're good at that, so for Mexico we may have to adopt a system in which our strength will be in defence. Hopefully the fans won't misinterpret it. If we're not going to be a team who score on a regular basis, we have to be good at everything else and we'll just have to be patient,' said Ferguson.

The Scots were the final qualifiers for the World Cup and they did not have to wait long to discover the identity of their opponents in Mexico. The draw on 15 December placed them in Group E with West Germany, Denmark and Uruguay, all three of whom appeared good enough to reach the final itself. Ferguson's assessment was realistic: 'We can't kid ourselves. This draw makes us fourth favourites in our group but that may well suit us.'

On 26 March, in a friendly against Romania, Dalglish, now 35, became the first Scot to win 100 caps. 'I would love to be in Mexico, playing in the finals for a fourth time,' he said. 'But I want to go on merit, not because of some sentimental gesture.' Before the game he performed a lap of honour after having been presented with a golden international cap by West German team manager Franz Beckenbauer. In front of 53,000 at Hampden, Dalglish was at his best, prompting the Scots to a sleek 3-0 victory. In Scotland's central defence, David Narey was alongside Willie Miller in the first half, then Hansen was beside Miller in the second half. Both partnerships looked solid. Beckenbauer said he had been impressed by Scotland's teamwork and by Strachan in particular. 'The group involving ourselves, Scotland, Denmark and Uruguay will be very close,' he said. 'There is nothing between all four sides and luck will play a big part in deciding who finishes in the first two.'

The Home Internationals had now been abandoned but the match with England had survived. Scotland were scheduled to play them at Wembley on 23 April, then a friendly in Holland on 29 April. Ferguson stated that those two matches would clarify his final decisions on the squad for the World Cup. Two scrappy goals gave England a 2-1 win and Ferguson his first defeat as Scotland team manager. Souness scored Scotland's goal with a penalty. In Eindhoven, a much-weakened Scotland side, depleted through call-offs, obtained a 0-0 draw. Scotland looked extremely slick and were denied good claims for a penalty in each half by Austrian referee Kohl. While in Holland, Ferguson, then 44, explained that he would be leaving the position as Scotland team manager after the World Cup. 'I'm too young for the job,' he said.

Mo Johnston had committed a breach of discipline while in Australia for the second leg of the play-off and was excluded from the World Cup squad. Charlie Nicholas was selected, even though he had played little part in the qualifiers, making only three substitute appearances. He was struggling to score goals at Arsenal. 'I may be criticized about Charlie Nicholas,' said Ferguson. 'But I'm sure he'll come good after five weeks with us. He's more like Dalglish and can do things few others can.'

Dalglish himself withdrew with a knee injury – two days before the Scotland squad

In front of 53,000 at Hampden, Dalglish was at his best, prompting the Scots to a sleek 3-0 victory.

flew out to North America for pre-tournament preparation. 'I feel I've let Fergie down,' said Dalglish, who, as player-manager, had, two days previously, led Liverpool to an FA Cup and League double. 'But ligaments have separated from my knee and I can't be fit in time.' Steve Archibald replaced him.

'Now I've got to rethink partnerships,' said Ferguson. 'My plan was to have a front two of Dalglish and McAvennie. People are looking for other reasons apart from injury for Kenny's withdrawal. This is nonsense. I know Dalglish and the way he spoke to me there's no doubt he was as disappointed as me. I've even been asked if Alan Hansen's non-selection had anything to do with it. Dalglish is out because of injury. He has damaged knee ligaments and a broken nose. There is no mystery about it.'

The Scots flew to Santa Fe, New Mexico – 7000ft above sea level – for two weeks of heat and altitude training. At altitude they would become used to the faster speed and different flight of the ball through the air. Before leaving, Ferguson had a two and a half hour meeting with Sir Alf Ramsey, who had managed the England team in Mexico in 1970. 'Sir Alf has kept a very detailed dossier from the last World Cup in Mexico. He gave me total access to it and it has proved really useful.'

Scotland warmed up in the USA with matches against Los Angeles Heat and Hollywood Kickers – all squad members were given a chance to play in both games. From there they travelled to Mexico which they reached on 1 June – the last country to arrive for the World Cup. Their first match would be three days later at the 35,000-capacity Neza stadium. Tickets for the matches there were selling slowly because of the Mexicans' fears of entering the area: Nezahualcoyotl was a vast slumland. Sights there shocked some of the Scottish squad as they passed through it on their way to the stadium.

Ferguson said: 'Michael Laudrup and Preben Elkjaer are brilliant. If we can stop them we've a great chance. My view is that if we get a result against the Danes we'll qualify. That's how important the first match is.' The encounter would take place in the late afternoon in Mexico, but at 11 p.m. British time. The Danes were in their first World Cup but their performances over the previous few years had established them as one of the world's premier international sides. Their manager Sepp Piontek believed strongly that they could win the World Cup. Their tussle with Scotland was to provide a thoroughly absorbing match. In the 12,000 crowd, there were 1,000 Scots.

Richard Gough (extreme right) puts a header over the bar during the match with Denmark in the 1986 World Cup finals. Paul Sturrock (second left) and members of the Tartan Army get a close look at the action.

Steve Nicol is tackled by Klaus Bergreen of Denmark.

The Scotland team line up before facing West Germany.

Scotland were first to come close to scoring. Nicholas used his chest to control a headed pass from Gough but his shot was blocked by a Danish defender close to goal. Nicholas again looked sprightly after ten minutes when he anticipated Sturrock's cross but his shot squeezed past a post. The Danes had only a couple of half-chances in the early stages. After 15 minutes, Gough's header zoomed over the bar. On the half-hour, Strachan, master of the expertly delayed pass, displayed that particular skill as he poked the ball into Gough's path but the right-back sent the ball over the bar when he should have managed to steer it between the Danish posts.

The best chance of the half, however, was created by the Danes. Arnesen passed to Elkjaer, took the return, but his shot cleared the post. The Danes opened the second half in the same fashion, this time Lerby's shot running close past the post. Elkjaer went even closer. Michael Laudrup's pass gave him time to assess his options and he took the ball past Leighton. The goalkeeper had, however, forced him to veer away from goal. When the striker got his bearings to shoot from a difficult angle, the ball streaked off the outside of a Scottish post. In the 57th minute, as the Danes kept the pressure on, Arnesen laid the ball into Elkjaer's path. On the edge of the penalty area, he hit the ball off Miller's shin, took it on and angled a shot away from Leighton. This time the ball hit the inside of the post and travelled over the goal-line.

Scotland reasserted themselves. A tricky shot from Strachan was held on the line by Rasmussen, the Danish goalkeeper, and Paul Sturrock had a shot that went only narrowly past. Closest of all came Aitken, whose measured strike from the edge of the Danish penalty area hit the net only to be given offside by Lajos Nemeth, the Hungarian referee. It looked a poor decision.

With ten minutes remaining, Nicholas dashed clear on goal and was immediately hacked down by Klaus Bergreen. The Dane was merely booked; Nicholas had to leave the field with damaged ankle ligaments. Earlier, McAvennie and Eamon Bannon had

replaced Sturrock and Strachan so Scotland had to play out the final minutes with ten men. In an interview after the game, Bergreen and Nicholas met up and the Dane, in the most civilized way, explained how, regrettably, he had had to hack down his 'friend'. Sturrock had also received an ankle injury.

'I thought we played well,' said Ferguson. 'I don't think I would want to single out anyone because I'm convinced everyone did what they could. We showed enough quality to do well in the next two games.' Sepp Piontek admitted that his team had been 'a little lucky' to win. The Neza stadium had been cool for Scotland's match with Denmark and the match had been played at a quick pace. The matches with West Germany and Uruguay would begin at noon. On Sunday 8 June, Scotland met West Germany at the Corregidora stadium in Queretaro with 25,000 fans sweltering in the heat.

Alex McLeish was ill before the game and was replaced in the centre of the Scottish defence by Narey. Archibald would be left on his own to look for any breaks that might come Scotland's way in front of goal. West Germany's side looked strong in every area. In just three minutes, Magath's cross found Allofs in front of goal. He headed the ball down towards the target but Leighton showed great suppleness to fly groundwards and steer the ball round the post. From the corner, Voller's header hit a Scottish post. On quarter of an hour, Archibald passed to Bannon. The wide man cut inside to shoot; the German goalkeeper Schumacher responded with agility, palming the ball over the bar.

Three minutes later, Gough found Aitken just outside the penalty area. He waited patiently before playing a fantastic pass into Strachan's path. The midfielder first-timed it past Schumacher to give Scotland a magnificent opening goal. In celebrating, the five foot six inches Strachan ran to an advertising board and lifted his leg on to the top of it. Earlier goal celebrations in the World Cup had seen players hurdling those boards; Strachan's joke was at the expense of his own height. Four minutes later, Allofs took a Littbarski pass on the left wing. His cross went to Voller who had taken up exactly the right position in front of goal. From there he kneed the ball past Leighton.

Scotland left-back Maurice Malpas's run and pass gave Souness time to shoot but the ball floated over the German goal. That was ten minutes before half-time. Five

Gordon Strachan sends a spectacular shot zipping into the German net for Scotland's only goal of the 1986 World Cup finals.

Steve Archibald is grounded and Frank McAvennie is crowded out as Scotland pressurize the German defence in their search for an equalizer.

Roy Aitken takes the ball round German central defender Klaus Augenthaler in the sweltering midday heat of Queretaro.

minutes on, Bannon's long-range free-kick crept through the German defensive wall but Schumacher made another accomplished save. The Germans looked to be playing slightly within themselves but Scotland, if they had some luck, still looked to be in with a chance of taking something from the game. To be drawing with such a strong side at half-time was highly encouraging. In the 50th minute, however, Narey attempted to clear while under pressure from Voller but the ball chopped off his shin straight to Allofs. He opened out his body and sent a 10-yard shot past Leighton.

Now the Germans went looking for the decisive goal but excellent saves by Leighton from Matthaus and Littbarski maintained Scottish hopes. Their resilience looked to have paid off when Strachan's corner was flicked on by Bannon to McAvennie, a substitute for Steve Nicol. The striker had sight of goal but miskicked. Cooper replaced Bannon and near the end the winger's cross reached Gough but his header sailed over the bar. Scotland had lost their last chance of retrieving a point.

The game had been played in a heat of 90 degrees and afterwards Souness commented: 'The general consensus among the players is that the conditions were the hardest they've ever had to play in. I felt all right until about 15 minutes into the second half and then it was difficult to make a run of any kind. The game really just died after that. It was reduced to walking pace, and the Germans were affected just as we were. It's a combination of heat and the altitude. I suppose teams such as Brazil and Mexico can cope with these conditions but really I doubt if the Europeans were here for even a year they would ever get completely used to it. All of the players suffered from weight loss, around 8lbs each. It's a hell of a way to lose weight.' One solution, of course, might have been to play matches in the cool of the evening. That, however, would not have suited European television schedulers.

Beckenbauer contrasted the 'good spirit' of this game with his side's match against Uruguay. He said: 'We knew and expected Scotland to be very good and so they were. They tested us severely. Strachan is a great player and we had a lot of difficulty keeping him under control.' Denmark had beaten Uruguay 6-1, a match in which Uruguay had Bossio sent off. 'We must keep our cool,' said Ferguson as he looked ahead to the encounter with Uruguay. 'The Uruguayan temperament let them down against the Danes and that could be in our favour on Friday. One advantage we have is that it is the last game of the qualifying series, and we will go into it knowing exactly what we have to do. I really do think Uruguay will worry about Strachan. He could be a vital man for us in that game.' Piontek said: 'I was concerned about the Uruguayans' toughness but fortunately the referee acted strongly. If that doesn't happen it could be difficult for Scotland.' A win and two points would make Scotland one of the four best third-placed teams who would proceed to the last 16. Uruguay were South American champions but after the disappointing result against Denmark rows were raging among the members of their squad and management over who should play.

With Souness having struggled badly in the opening two games he was replaced by Paul McStay, the talented central midfielder from Celtic. He was just 21 but possessed an extremely calm temperament. Graeme Sharp, the Everton striker, replaced Archibald. Ferguson had used the fifth of his five forwards. Inside the first minute Jose Batista saw red and launched himself at Strachan's legs. He immediately saw red again as the French referee, Joel Quiniou, produced the card that sent him from the field. The Uruguayans, however, were used to playing with ten men and for the rest of the game the referee seemed to retreat from his earlier strict stance, perhaps for fear of seeming over-harsh on the Uruguayans. Consequently, a series of fouls on Strachan throughout the match went unpunished.

Francescoli, the Uruguayans' most potent forward, had the first real chance of the match. He evaded several thumping tackles and sent in a shot that Leighton saved close to his post. Cabrera and Francescoli had further opportunities for Uruguay but after 18 minutes Aitken smacked a low cross to Nicol in front of goal. From six yards, he failed to get any purchase on his shot and Alvez saved. In that moment, many Scots sensed despair. The Uruguayans' fouling prevented Scotland finding any rhythm. The Scots also appeared to lack the level of guile needed to deal with the Uruguayans' tactics. After the referee blew the whistle for half-time he was surrounded and jostled by Uruguayans. FIFA officials had to rescue him from their attentions.

Referee Joel Quiniou sends off Uruguay's Batista (on ground) after his foul tackle on Strachan in the first minute of the match between Scotland and Uruguay.

Strachan's clever football in Scotland's earlier matches had ensured he would be the recipient of some tough treatment from the Uruguayans. For the 89 minutes after Batista's sending-off he was pushed, pulled and pummelled all over the pitch.

Alex Ferguson struggles to contain his anger after the match with Uruguay had produced a frustrating anti-climax to the 1986 World Cup for Scotland. Ferguson was appointed manager of Manchester United in November 1986, five months after taking Scotland to the World Cup finals.

Midway through the second half, Leighton did exceptionally well to tip a Cabrera header over the bar. Sturrock had the ball in the Uruguayan net but was given offside. Gough and Narey went close but the game petered out frustratingly in a 0-0 draw; the result the Uruguayans had wanted. There were some strong words spoken after this game. 'As a nation Uruguay seem to have no respect for anyone,' was Ferguson's opinion. 'That was a débâcle out there. I know we are out of the World Cup but honestly I am glad to be going home because this is no way to play football.'

Ernie Walker, a man who normally appeared likely to get upset only over something like the air-conditioning in his hotel, said: 'We found ourselves on the field with cheats and cowards. We were associated with the scum of world football and if anybody thinks that had anything to do with football it's news to me.'

Scotland had been extremely unfortunate. Certainly they had been outplayed by the Germans but the two 'offside' goals in the matches against Denmark and Uruguay could have given them the extra point they needed to qualify. Ferguson had been thrown into the job unexpectedly and later admitted he had been too inexperienced for the task. The loss of Dalglish had been a major blow and, just as Ferguson's faith in Nicholas was being rewarded by rejuvenated performances from the player, he was struck down by a viciously inflicted injury, compounded by his looking almost certain to score at the time. From then, Scotland were rarely convincing as an attacking force.

Despite the handicap of the heat, Scotland had made a finer contribution, in their own small way, to the World Cup than had Uruguay who, before the tournament began, had been one of the favourites to take the trophy itself. However, Scotland, had they qualified from their group, would have shared the Uruguayans' forthcoming fate. In the first match of the knockout phase they lost to Argentina.

It was the end of an era: Souness and Dalglish had played their final World Cup games for Scotland. The next Scottish party to tackle a World Cup would be of a radically different nature.

THE NEW REALISM
ITALY, 1990

'I need players who will compete, men who will run. But even that won't be enough. We will have to damage them.'

Andy Roxburgh before Scotland v Sweden, 1990

Andy Roxburgh had been on the staff of the Scottish Football Association for ten years when he was promoted to national coach in July 1986. His was a name well-known to fellow coaches but to the wider Scottish public he was an unknown quantity.

Andy Roxburgh, Scotland's team manager for the 1990 World Cup finals, was noted for his meticulous planning and attention to detail. However, even he, in his pre-match assessment, was unlikely to have noted the potential significance of the dugouts being situated directly opposite the dressing-rooms at the Luigi Ferraris Stadium, Genoa. That only really became obvious after his side had lost 1-0 to Costa Rica there, in Scotland's first 90 minutes of the 1990 World Cup. As Roxburgh strode across the width of the pitch from dugout to dressing-room, the 10,000 Scots in the 30,000 crowd bellowed their boos, many screeching at him in the strongest terms to resign there and then.

Roxburgh's immediate post-match assessment was: 'We made so many chances – all we needed was one to go in the net. These things happen in football: sometimes the counter-attacking team steals the match. Their goalkeeper had a great game and we just couldn't finish. Costa Rica played the way they are capable of playing and one or two of ours weren't as good as they should have been. We were hammering into them non-stop and the thing just wouldn't go in the back of the net for us. I'm afraid that's football. Dame Fortune was on their side rather than ours. You can't guarantee you are going to win. I said all along it would be an awkward and difficult game for us. They scored on the break and that was it – we couldn't equalize.'

On returning to the Hotel Bristol, the Scots' base close to Rapallo, video evidence would have shown him that those comments were not fully justified. Certainly Scotland had more chances than Costa Rica but they had done nothing that had matched the Costa Ricans' goal. It came five minutes after half-time. Chavez picked the ball up on the halfway line, exchanged passes with Jara and moved inside. He passed to Ramirez who switched the ball, in turn, to Marchena. The ball had now travelled in style from left to right wing. Marchena was confronted by Maurice Malpas but he bided his time, feinted very slightly to go to his right and wrongfooted the left-back. There was just enough room for Marchena to edge past Malpas. He then stroked the ball inside to Jara who had expertly moved off Dave McPherson's shoulder at exactly the right moment. A quick back-heel from Jara left Stuart McKimmie floundering. The ball moved on to Cayasso who first-timed a left-footed flick over the diving Jim Leighton. It was a goal of some sophistication. Shortly afterwards an almost identical but abbreviated version of this move caught Scotland out again. This time it ended with a Jara shot being saved by Leighton.

After that, Alan McInally headed over with the target begging him to hit it and a Mo Johnston shot was blocked by Conejo at close range. Scotland also won a couple of free-kicks in promising positions. But for all Roxburgh's famed preparations, it was puzzling that the coach hadn't imparted more to his side on what to do in such

Paul McStay goes for the ball in the air with Roger Gomez of Costa Rica. Scotland's defeat to the Costa Ricans surprised most watchers of the 1990 World Cup. The Central Americans, playing in their first World Cup finals, were, however, a well-coached, skilful side. They consolidated their early success against Scotland by defeating Sweden 2-1 to qualify for the knockout stages of the tournament where they lost to Czechoslovakia.

situations. Both kicks were directly in front of the Costa Rican goal. For the first, Jim Bett, who was having an appalling game, blootered the ball high and wide. For the second, McPherson, a gangly, awkward central defender, stepped up to slice the ball many yards wide of goal.

As the culmination of Roxburgh's four years of work with the national team, it wasn't much of a result. On 16 July 1986 he had been picked by the SFA to be the new national coach. At the time he was 42 and had been on the SFA staff as a coach since 1976. A former player with Queen's Park, Falkirk, Partick Thistle and Clydebank, he had also been a primary school headmaster before joining the SFA. He had an impressive record as coach of Scottish teams at various levels. On 30 May 1982, shortly before the World Cup finals in Spain, the Scotland Under–18s, coached and managed by Roxburgh, had beaten Czechoslovakia 3-1 to win the European Championship for Under-18s. At the time of his appointment, he was the SFA's Director of Coaching. In June 1986, Roxburgh had been in Guadalajara as one of FIFA's official representatives and match observers for the World Cup finals group involving Brazil, Spain, Northern Ireland and Algeria.

'I was stunned when I was asked,' Roxburgh said of his appointment. 'But when you get an opportunity like this you can't turn it down. I have supervised the young team inside a packed Aztec stadium so I know what the pressures can be like.' Ernie Walker commented: 'We felt it was not a bad idea for a change from the past and we feel confident we have the right man for the job. The old method whereby the manager was chosen from without has not been entirely successful, and the committee felt that this was the opportunity to start afresh with the man in charge being in-house, as it were.'

It was the beginning of a new system whereby the SFA would groom its future managerial and coaching staff for the national team. Craig Brown was to be Roxburgh's assistant.

Scotland's journey through the World Cup qualifiers had started at a brisk pace but had then become slow and tortuous. In the autumn of 1988, after a solid 2-1 win over Norway in Oslo, they drew 1-1 with Yugoslavia in Glasgow. That match was watched by 42,771, the lowest crowd for a World Cup match in Scotland since a tie with Cyprus in 1969. In February 1989, the Scots renewed World Cup acquaintance with the Cypriots in Limassol. A Richard Gough header – six minutes into stoppage time at the end of the match – gave Scotland a 3-2 win.

Scotland then prepared to meet the remaining team in the group, France, at Hampden. A win for Scotland would give them seven points out of eight and would leave the French, erratic until then, struggling to make one of the two qualifying places in the group. Beforehand, Michel Platini, the French manager, uttered a Jacques Brel-like *cri de coeur*: 'I have no one. There is no one to stop the game. I don't have a player who can put a foot on the ball and distribute it.'

Roxburgh was more prosaic: 'Although this match is not a last-ditch game it represents an important crossroads. This match can send us in the right direction and the French the wrong way. No matter what happens no one can say it's over. Neither team will be home and dry, or finished.' On the Monday before the match, Roxburgh and Brown arranged for the Under-21 side to adopt the French formation and approach in a training game. The first eleven won 2-0.

The Scotland side that took the field for the game on 8 March 1989 was: Leighton, Gough, Malpas, Aitken, McLeish, Gillespie, Nicol, McStay, McCoist, Ferguson, Johnston. It was a dreadful, rain-sodden night but 65,000 turned out on Hampden Park terraces that remained largely uncovered. It was the final spectacular at the old-style Hampden, soon to be conquered by civilization in the form of an all-seater, all-covered arena. The first notable chance fell to France. Laurey's shot had Leighton stretching low to turn the ball round his post. Ally McCoist and Johnston, the Scottish forwards, were being systematically battered by their opponents in the French defence. But Paul McStay, Aitken and Steve Nicol formed a hard-headed, practical midfield and if the strikers could cope with their pain, opportunities seemed sure to appear for them.

Maurice Johnston turns away after his second goal against France had put Scotland in an exceptionally strong position to qualify for the 1990 World Cup finals. Johnston, then playing for Nantes, received death threats in France in the wake of his two goals in Scotland's 2-0 win.

With almost half an hour gone, Scotland got the required goal. McCoist directed the ball towards the French goal. Johnston intercepted it, stunned it, then, showing great nerve, sidefooted it with precision past French goalkeeper Bats. Eight minutes after half-time Johnston met Nicol's cross for a header that Bats clawed at but couldn't prevent creeping inside the post.

As the French revived, Papin brought a fine save out of Leighton, as did Battiston from a free-kick. The rebound dropped neatly for Papin whose shot looked a sure goal until Leighton made the most accomplished save of the night.

From goalkeeper to striker it had been an evening of commitment and endeavour. It had been a dedicated, workmanlike performance from Scotland although the team lacked the inspirational qualities of Scotland teams of the past. 'I am pleased for the lads because they have taken some stick. We've said all along we are not world beaters but we have good spirit and we try to be well-organized. It is easy for Scottish people to get carried away, but we must control ourselves and get on with it,' was Roxburgh's assessment.

Johnston executes a perfect overhead kick to score against Cyprus at Hampden in the World Cup qualifying match in April 1989.

The following month, a perfectly executed overhead kick from Johnston proved the winning goal as Scotland struggled to beat Cyprus 2-1 at Hampden. It broke the previous World Cup scoring record of seven goals held jointly by Joe Jordan and Kenny Dalglish. The players' match fees and the gate receipts from the 50,000 crowd were donated to the Hillsborough disaster fund, set up after the deaths of 94 Liverpool fans at the FA Cup semi-final in Sheffield 18 days previously.

Johnston had scored in all five of Scotland's World Cup ties in the 1988–89 season. Since moving to Nantes in France from Celtic in 1987 he had become a more perceptive player. He was more tactically aware and, after the technically refined but atmospherically depressurized French football, he must have relished his occasional return visits to Scotland.

Scotland now entered their final three games with nine points from a possible ten. In Zagreb in September, against Yugoslavia, Durie gave Scotland a first-half lead with a canny header. But, inspired by the brilliance of Dragan Stojkovic, the Yugoslavs hit back to win 3-1. Two of their goals were own goals, one by Nicol, one by Gillespie, the other a terrible misjudgement by Leighton who was performing poorly for his club, Manchester United.

In Paris in October, the French trounced the Scots 3-0. Eric Cantona was among the goalscorers as the Scots were played off the park by a French team who looked as though they could contribute a great deal more to the World Cup finals, if they qualified, than Scotland.

Those results meant that, as Scotland went into their final match of the qualifying series, at home to Norway, they needed a point to qualify for Italia '90. They had scored 11 goals and conceded 11. A win for Norway would leave France only needing to beat Cyprus to go through. Roxburgh was in positive mood before the match: 'Scots fans love drama and that's what Wednesday is all about. It will be a thriller or a tragedy. However, I see no reason why we should be pessimistic.' The match had been sold out several weeks previously although the new capacity of Hampden was 64,000 in those post-Hillsborough days.

A minute before half-time, Malpas headed the ball forward down the inside-left channel and McCoist touched it high over the head of Thorstvedt in the Norway goal to make it 1-0 to Scotland. The score remained the same until the 90th minute when the Norwegian defender Erland Johnsen hit the ball forward from just inside the Scotland half and wide on the right wing. Amazingly, Leighton fumbled it and the ball slipped over the line to create a nerve-ridden final few seconds. But they passed,

Ally McCoist shows the joy of scoring for Scotland after his goal had given the Scots the lead in their vital World Cup tie with Norway in November 1989.

eventually, and Scotland were in the World Cup finals for the fifth consecutive time.

Scotland contested five friendlies before the finals. In March 1990, at Hampden, a memorable McKimmie goal gave them a 1-0 win over world champions Argentina. In April they lost 1-0 at home to East Germany. An appalling performance against Egypt at Pittodrie in May saw Scotland lose 3-1. Egypt's second goal had been created by Durie; his high cross back towards his own goal was headed over Scotland goalkeeper Brian Gunn by Hossam Hassan. 'We must eradicate these freak accidents,' said Roxburgh. 'We've had a horrendous season of our own people taking brainstorms.'

A friendly with Poland at Hampden continued Scotland's glut of own goals, Gillespie grabbing his second of the season in the 1-1 draw. Johnston was the scorer for Scotland. On 24 May, the players flew to Malta for a week's acclimatization and training. They would also play their final pre-World Cup friendly, against the Maltese national side.

In Malta, Roxburgh said that the players would be banned from drinking from then, 25 May. 'It starts now and will go on as long as we're in the World Cup. There are two reasons for this. The first is medical, but we want also to wipe out the image of whisky-swilling footballers. It has never been true but countries have reputations for doing certain things and ours is drinking whisky. It's grossly unfair and as one who has never had a glass of whisky, I find it offensive. I don't think many, if any, of the players drink spirits. They take beer or lager. To me, booze isn't right in a football context. Bevvy dehydrates and this is what we want to avoid. The lads have accepted the ban without any hassle.' It was intriguing to wonder what Whyte & Mackay, the official sponsors of Scotland's World Cup qualifying matches, made of this.

> '*On paper the next two games, against Sweden and Brazil, are much harder but you can't apply logic to Scotland.*'

Another headed own goal, this time from McPherson, gave Malta their goal in Scotland's 2-1 win. McInally scored twice to give the Scots two wins in eight games over the season – Scotland had scored five own goals in those games.

On 31 May the players returned to Scotland and, after five days at home, the squad flew to Italy. Scotland's new age of realism was confirmed by the bookmakers: William Hill had them at 50-1 to take the World Cup. Italy were favourites at 3-1 with West Germany at 7-1.

In Scotland's opening match, both the Scots and Costa Rica had played in a very polite fashion – neither side had sustained any bookings. Scotland's approach had to be more aggressive against Sweden. 'We mustn't think it's all over for us,' said Roxburgh. 'On paper the next two games, against Sweden and Brazil, are much harder but you can't apply logic to Scotland.' Looking ahead to the Sweden game, he declared: 'I need players who will compete, men who will run. But even that won't be enough. My players must cause Sweden problems. We will have to damage them.'

Roxburgh had watched Brazil, Costa Rica and Sweden three times each before the World Cup but there was little that World Cup managers did not know about each other's sides in the 1990s, the age of omnipresent media. By the time of the 1990 World Cup, satellite television had arrived: Eurosport had live coverage of all Scotland's games. Grampian and STV had the Costa Rica and Brazil games live with highlights of the Swedish game. The BBC had the Swedish game live with highlights of Brazil and Costa Rica; Radio 2 and Radio Scotland broadcast commentary on all of Scotland's games, as did local radio stations. Fans could also watch recorded games endlessly on their video recorders. Increased media attention meant more money for competing countries and the SFA would make around £2 million from the first round while the players would share £250,000. Bonuses for reaching later rounds and match fees had all been smoothly sorted out by the SFA.

Before the match with Sweden, thousands of Scots and Swedes joined in a parade that wound its way from the centre of Genoa to the stadium as the Tartan Army enhanced its reputation in yet another country. Again, there would be no arrests of

Scottish fans throughout a World Cup tournament. Sweden had also lost their first game, 2-1 to Brazil in Turin, and anticipated quite a battle. By kick-off time that muggy summer evening, Genoa's magnificent Luigi Ferraris Stadium was awash with tension – defeat for either side would make further World Cup progress very difficult. Andy Roxburgh made changes in all areas of the team. In the absence of the injured Richard Gough, central defender Dave McPherson was moved to the right-hand side of defence while Craig Levein came in for McPherson in the middle. Paul McStay and Jim Bett were replaced by two more direct, physical midfielders in Murdo MacLeod and Gordon Durie. There was a change of striking partner for Mo Johnston, with Robert Fleck replacing McInally.

The Scots in the crowd outnumbered the Swedes and made their presence felt appropriately. As their team had stumbled to defeat during the Costa Rican encounter, some Scottish fans were seen tearing up their tickets for the match with Sweden and vowing they would head for home immediately. Yet far from there being a backlash from the Costa Rica game, the supporters appeared determined to show their patriotism was as strong as ever. The importance of the Tartan Army was tacitly acknowledged by Andy Roxburgh. He crossed the field to the dugout wearing a smart SFA suit but with a tartan scarf draped around his neck. 'We've got to be positive and go for the win,' said Roy Aitken beforehand. 'It might be the first end-to-end match of the tournament. We are sure we're better than them – now we have to prove it.'

The game began at a furious pace and both sides showed their determination through some particularly hard tackling. In the third minute, Sweden's Schwarz whipped a shot narrowly over the bar. But Durie and Fleck began to trouble the Swedes with their clever running and the fans enjoyed a sparky opening ten minutes. The Scots were further cheered when their team won a corner. MacLeod's kick was flicked on at the near post by McPherson, the ball dropped close to the goal-line and McCall, amidst a jam of bodies, prodded the ball past Ravelli. Bewilderment registered among the Scottish fans as to how a side that had taken only ten minutes to penetrate one of Europe's most highly rated defences had been unable earlier to beat Costa Rica.

The first half ended with neither of Sweden's front two, Brolin and Pettersson, having had a serious attempt at goal and the Scottish team went into the dressing room with their ears ringing to the sound of fanatical applause. They had already more than made up for their insipid showing against Costa Rica. The atmosphere was right for a light-hearted half-time episode as substitutes Ally McCoist and Bryan Gunn took souvenir photographs of each other in front of the Scottish support.

Ten minutes after half-time Brolin finally came alive with a searing run down the left side of the field. For the first time in the match he managed to shake off the Scottish defence but Leighton did well to hold the striker's powerful shot. Late in the second half, McStay replaced Durie, who left the field to a standing ovation from the Scottish fans. The final ten minutes were to surpass all that had gone before. A perfectly weighted pass from McStay in the 80th minute sent Johnston clear, only for the striker to be foiled by Schwarz's lunging tackle. A minute later, Fleck slipped the ball into space behind the Swedish defence. The Scots' much-criticized captain, Roy Aitken, showed his pace to outstrip the Swedish defenders as they struggled to turn and keep up with play. Ravelli blocked the big man's first shot but, as Aitken went to slot the rebound into the empty net, he was tripped from behind by Roland Nilsson. Johnston confidently smashed the penalty-kick high into Ravelli's net.

Four minutes from time Sweden pulled a goal back. The Scottish defence seemed to freeze as Roland Nilsson's long, high ball soared over them and fell for Stromberg to stretch the point of his boot at the ball and squirt it into the Scottish net. That goal sparked off frenetic Swedish pursuit of an equalizer. With a minute left a 30-yard free-kick from Schwarz went just wide of Leighton's left-hand post. Then, in the dying seconds, Stromberg just failed to connect with another Roland Nilsson pass.

Scotland held on. They had rewarded their tortured supporters with a display of unexpected spirit, application and coordination. They now had an excellent chance to proceed to the knockout stages of the tournament. The normally reserved Roxburgh

(overleaf)
Stuart McCall prods the ball over the Swedish line for Scotland's opening goal in the 1990 World Cup finals. Mo Johnston (extreme left) and Alex McLeish (extreme right) turn away in delight while Robert Fleck (number 13) rushes towards the scorer (partially hidden on the ground). Craig Levein (number 6) celebrates from the halfway line.

waved his scarf in triumph as he crossed the pitch to the dressing-room. Jim Leighton showed his delight with exuberant gestures in the direction of the Scottish supporters.

Roxburgh's tactics had been precise to the point of perfection. The Swedes had been perceived as being weak at full-back and Durie and Fleck had been brought in to test the Swedes in precisely that area of the field. Durie used his pace and power on the left wing while the Swedes could not pin down Fleck as he went bobbing and weaving down the right. A score of chances were created as the Swedish defence toiled to cope with the unpredictable and varied Scottish attacks. The Scottish defence was also a more compact unit thanks largely to McPherson and Levein's masterly reading of the play. In midfield, the harrying presence of Aitken and MacLeod gave the Scots an edge of steel.

The Scottish team went into the dressing room with their ears ringing to the sound of fanatical applause

The Scots, now in second place in the group, moved to Saint Vincent in the Italian Alps before the ultimate test, against Brazil in Turin. The Brazilians had beaten Costa Rica 1-0 but had struggled to do it. Again a Brazilian manager, Sebastião Lazaroni, was imposing a European style of play on the team. Pelé and many other vocal critics had expressed a desire to see Brazil play with three up front. Their young striker Romario said: 'Pelé is right. Lazaroni is making mistakes with this line-up and Brazil cannot win the World Cup playing like this.'

With the win over Costa Rica, Brazil had already qualified from the group but if they finished first there was the chance they would play Argentina. It was rumoured they wished second place to manoeuvre themselves into an easier tie. That prompted Lazaroni to say: 'I had planned to rest almost the whole team but I changed my mind after false speculation in Brazil that we did not want to win the group.' Romario, despite his comments, came in to replace Muller in the Brazilian attack.

Warm rain streamed down all day and all evening, as the Turin trams brought the fans to the resplendent Stadio Delle Alpi, built to order for the World Cup. A crowd of 62,000 generated receipts of £1.8 million.

Levein, absent with a thigh injury, was replaced by McKimmie, who came in at right-back with McPherson moving back into central defence. Johnston was booked in the fifth minute for a stupid, unnecessary foul on Ricardo Rocha. MacLeod suffered the same fate in the seventh minute for a foul on Jorginho. In the opening quarter of

Mo Johnston puts Scotland into a 2-0 lead in their match with Sweden in Genoa. After the 1990 World Cup, Johnston surprisingly announced his retirement from international football at the age of 27. He made a brief comeback the following year before finally deciding he no longer wished to play for the Scottish national team.

an hour, the only other incident of any note was a Branco free-kick from 20 yards that knocked Johnston over as it crashed into the Scottish defensive wall. Otherwise, neither side had come close to having a shot or header on target.

Even from high in the Stadio Delle Alpi stands, it was impossible to assess the Brazilian formation, so fluid were they in their movement. They were also swift to flash into attack. When an enormous kickout by Leighton almost went as far as the Brazilian penalty area, Ricardo Gomes climbed to head it to Valdo. He smartly rolled it from one foot to the other before smoothing his way past three Scottish players in the midfield. His pass was picked up by Romario, who now had only McLeish between him and Leighton. The striker – playing his first match since breaking a leg playing for his club side PSV Eindhoven the previous March – opted to turn the ball out to Jorginho on the right wing. His instantaneous cross swirled over the Scottish six-yard box where it was almost headed into his own goal by McKimmie. Branco's corner curved over Leighton's head but, stretching backwards, the Scottish goalkeeper tipped the ball away as Romario waited at the back post.

Even from high in the Stadio Delle Alpi stands, it was impossible to assess the ever-fluid Brazilian formation

Scotland recovered themselves for a couple of minutes before being split open again when Dunga curved a magnificent pass with the outside of his right boot deep into the Scottish half. Alemão swiftly switched it inside but Aitken clipped the ball away before it reached Careca, poised in front of goal.

After 20 minutes, Scotland created their first half-chance. Aitken won the ball in the air and found MacLeod with his header. Johnston, who had moved to wide on the left wing, crossed into the Brazilian box where the ball skidded off McCoist's forehead but well wide of the Brazilian goal. It was significant that Scotland's first threatening move had come from the use of the wing. Fleck and Durie, who had powered wide to such strong effect against Sweden, were on the substitutes' bench for the Brazil game. Yet the Brazilians looked as though they would be less than comfortable if they were tested in those areas. As it was, Johnston and McCoist, Scotland's two forwards, were lost in a maze of yellow shirts in their central roles.

Another Branco free-kick sent MacLeod flying – the midfielder needed several minutes' treatment and eventually had to be replaced by Gillespie. The first attempt on target from either side was a Ricardo Gomes snap shot after the ball had fallen loose to him at a corner. It was easily held by Leighton. Other than McCoist's early effort, the only other opening that Scotland created in the first half came when McCall stretched the Brazilians again on the wing – again McCoist just failed to connect with McCall's hard-hit cross.

The match continued to smoulder up to and after half-time, the Scots rarely straying near the vicinity of the Brazilian penalty box, the Brazilians easing forward constantly but rarely able to progress past the Scots' 18-yard line. With almost an hour gone, however, a sublime Brazilian move exploded out of nothing. Branco, finding his way blocked by McStay, backheeled the ball yards behind himself then reversed on to it. That provided him with a chink of light through the curtain of the Scottish defence. He stabbed the ball forward to Careca, bypassing three Scots in the process. Careca, on the turn, pulled the curtain wide with a sweetly spun pass with the outside of his boot which took out another three Scots. It also gave Romario a clear-as-daylight view of goal as the striker went racing between Gillespie and McPherson. His scooped shot was goalbound but Leighton, fast off his line, spread himself well and held on to the ball.

That magnificent move, which had sliced open the centre of the Scots' defence, showed them the danger of their high-risk defensive policy. It also showed that this Brazilian side was as creative as their predecessors. The next notable move for Romario, however, was to be substituted by Muller in the 65th minute. The Scots did appear to take heed of the warning. A glimmer of hope shone Scotland's way when

McStay and McCall combined cleverly deep in the Scots' half. McCall's perceptive through-ball played McCoist in behind the last Brazilian defender but the ball fled from his foot as he attempted to control it. And with 15 minutes remaining, Aitken met McCall's corner with a clean header that Branco cleared off the Brazilian line with goalkeeper Taffarel beaten.

With seven minutes remaining, McStay did well to anticipate a Careca pass on the edge of the Scotland penalty area. But the midfielder's subsequent pass was disappointing. It went to Ricardo Gomes, the Brazilian captain, just inside the Scots' half. He moved the ball to Branco, wide on the left wing, who brought it back inside again and sent the ball to Alemão who had found space just outside the penalty area. He knocked a low shot towards Leighton's goal which ground off both the slippery surface and Leighton's chest. The ball lingered briefly on the edge of the six-yard box as Leighton, Gillespie and Careca all converged on it. As they twisted in a heap, the ball angled away from their combined collapse. It was running slowly past Leighton's post until Muller, at the last second, tapped it into the unguarded net to put Brazil ahead.

With less than a minute remaining, Johnston had a goalbound shot blocked, then Valdo sped upfield and passed to Alemão whose close-range shot was turned behind by Leighton. The subsequent corner having been tidied up by the Scots, it was their turn to attack as stoppage time ticked away. Johnston passed inside to Roy Aitken who set McKimmie up for a cross to the back post that Mauro Galvão could only head as far as Malpas on the edge of the Brazilian penalty area. His header went to Fleck who twisted on to the ball but failed to get any purchase on it and it bounced to Johnston right on the edge of the six-yard box. His shot was speeding towards the net until Taffarel got the merest touch on it to divert the ball over the bar. It left Scottish fans wondering what the outcome of this game might have been if the Scots had shown such fiery initiative from the first minute.

Roxburgh said: 'We lost because people were getting tired. Saturday's game against Sweden had taken a lot out of us and when players are tired mistakes are made.' Lazaroni commented: 'I thought Scotland were quite good but we played well. We had the patience to wait for a goal and our rhythm was faster in the second half.' Before

The Scottish team on the Turin turf before the encounter with Brazil that would decide whether they would progress from the group stage at the 1990 World Cup.

(opposite)
Two young fans, one Brazilian, one Scottish, enjoying the atmosphere in the Stadio Delle Alpi, Turin.

the match, a draw had been expected to take the Scots through with three points in second place: it was still presumed that the Costa Ricans' result against Scotland had been a fluke and that they would lose to Sweden. Instead, the Central Americans had defeated the Swedes in a match played simultaneously with the Scotland–Brazil one.

Scotland were now hoping to go through as one of the four best third-placed teams. They watched anxiously the following day as Uruguay took on South Korea. Uruguay needed a win to go through in third place. The game remained 0-0 until the Uruguayans scored in the third minute of stoppage time. In the evening, Scotland's last chance slowly faded away as the Republic of Ireland and Holland strolled through a 1-1 draw that they knew would send them both through.

On their return, the Scottish squad got a polite welcome home from around 200 holidaymakers who happened to be passing through Glasgow airport at that time. The fans, who were making their way home from Italy, had memories of that World Cup which would burn brightly throughout the 1990s and beyond. The despondency that followed the unexpected defeat by Costa Rica had made the equally unexpected win over Sweden all the sweeter. The match with Brazil had been another great occasion. Those and other World Cup memories would inspire Scotland teams and supporters in future years as they aimed to add to Scotland's notable contribution to the greatest competition on earth.

(opposite, top) Mo Johnston shoots for goal in the final minute of the match with Brazil.

(opposite, bottom) Taffarel, the Brazilian goalkeeper, gets a slight deflection on the ball to divert it inches over his bar.

(below) The Brazilians watch the ball as it flies into obscurity. Johnston, his last reserves of energy spent, stretches out on the turf, a figure of despair.

FACTS AND FIGURES

WORLD CUP 1954, SWITZERLAND

SCOTLAND WORLD CUP SQUAD: Martin *(Aberdeen)*, Aird *(Burnley)*, Cunningham *(Preston)*, Docherty *(Preston)*, Cowie *(Dundee)*, Davidson *(Partick Thistle)*, Evans *(Celtic)*, McKenzie *(Partick Thistle)*, Johnstone *(Hibs)*, Brown *(Blackpool)*, Mochan *(Celtic)*, Fernie *(Celtic)*, Ormond *(Hibs)*

SCOTLAND 0 AUSTRIA 1
16 June, 1954, Zurich:
Martin, Cunningham, Aird, Docherty, Davidson, Cowie, McKenzie, Fernie, Mochan, Brown, Ormond

SCOTLAND 0 URUGUAY 7
19 June, 1954, Basle:
Martin, Cunningham, Aird, Docherty, Davidson, Cowie, McKenzie, Fernie, Mochan, Brown, Ormond

For the first time in the World Cup finals, 16 teams participated. At the group stages, the two seeded countries played the two unseeded countries only. Two teams qualified for the quarter-finals from each of the four groups. After qualifying from Scotland's group, Uruguay defeated England 4-2 in the quarter-finals but lost 4-2 to Hungary in the semis. Austria defeated Switzerland 7-5 in the quarter-finals but lost 6-1 to West Germany in the semis. In the third/fourth place play-off, Austria beat Uruguay 3-1. In the final, Hungary, who had beaten the Germans 8-3 in the group stages, lost 3-2 despite having gone into a 2-0 lead in the opening ten minutes.

1954 World Cup final: Hungary 2 West Germany 3, Berne, 60,000

Top scorer in tournament: Sandor Kocsis (Hungary) 11 goals

WORLD CUP 1958, SWEDEN

SCOTLAND WORLD CUP SQUAD: Younger *(Liverpool)*, Brown *(Dundee)*, Caldow *(Rangers)*, Turnbull *(Hibs)*, Leggat *(Aberdeen)*, Murray *(Hearts)*, Hewie *(Charlton Athletic)*, Cowie *(Dundee)*, Collins *(Celtic)*, Imlach *(Nottingham Forest)*, Parker *(Everton)*, Docherty *(Preston North End)*, Scott *(Rangers)*, Baird *(Rangers)*, Haddock *(Clyde)*, Mackay *(Hearts)*, Robertson *(Clyde)*, Fernie *(Celtic)*, Evans *(Celtic)*, McColl *(Rangers)*, Mudie *(Blackpool)*, Coyle *(Clyde)*

SCOTLAND 1 YUGOSLAVIA 1
8 June 1958, Vasteras:
Younger, Hewie, Caldow, Turnbull, Evans, Cowie, Leggat, Collins, Mudie, Murray, Imlach

SCOTLAND 2 PARAGUAY 3
11 June 1958, Norrköping:
Younger, Parker, Caldow, Turnbull, Evans, Cowie, Leggat, Collins, Mudie, Robertson, Fernie

SCOTLAND 1 FRANCE 2
15 June, Orebro:
Brown, Caldow, Hewie, Turnbull, Evans, Mackay, Collins, Murray, Mudie, Baird, Imlach

As in the Swiss finals, there would be four groups of four with the top two in each group progressing to the quarter-finals. This time, each team would play all three others in their group. In the quarter-finals, Yugoslavia lost 1–0 to West Germany who, in turn, lost to Sweden in the semis. France beat Northern Ireland 4-0 to reach the semis where they lost 5-2 to Brazil. France beat West Germany 6-3 in the third/fourth place play-off. In the final, the 17-year-old Pelé scored twice as Brazil beat the hosts 5-2 to win their first World Cup.

1958 World Cup final: Brazil 5 Sweden 2, Stockholm, 49,737

Top scorer in tournament: Just Fontaine (France) 13 goals

WORLD CUP 1974, WEST GERMANY

SCOTLAND WORLD CUP SQUAD: Harvey *(Leeds United)*, Allan *(Dundee)*, Stewart *(Kilmarnock)*, Jardine *(Rangers)*, McGrain *(Celtic)*, Bremner *(Leeds United)*, Holton *(Manchester United)*, Blackley *(Hibs)*, Johnstone *(Celtic)*, Dalglish *(Celtic)*, Jordan *(Leeds United)*, Hay *(Celtic)*, Lorimer *(Leeds United)*, Buchan *(Manchester United)*, Cormack *(Liverpool)*, Donachie *(Manchester City)*, Hutchison *(Coventry City)*, Ford *(Hearts)*, Law *(Manchester City)*, Morgan *(Manchester United)*, McQueen *(Leeds United)*, Schaedler *(Hibs)*

SCOTLAND 2 ZAIRE 0
Dortmund, 12 June 1974:
Harvey, Jardine, McGrain, Bremner, Holton, Blackley, Lorimer, Dalglish (Hutchison), Jordan, Hay, Law

SCOTLAND 0 BRAZIL 0
Frankfurt, 16 June 1974:
Harvey, Jardine, McGrain, Holton, Buchan, Bremner, Hay, Dalglish, Morgan, Jordan, Lorimer

SCOTLAND 1 YUGOSLAVIA 1
Frankfurt, 20 June 1974:
Harvey, Jardine, McGrain, Buchan, Holton, Bremner, Hay, Dalglish (Hutchison), Morgan, Jordan, Lorimer

The first round would consist of four groups of four. The top two qualified for the last eight but there were no quarter-finals or semi-finals. Instead the second round consisted of two groups of four. The winner of each group would contest the final. In the last eight, Yugoslavia lost all three of their matches, to West Germany, Sweden and Poland. Brazil defeated East Germany and Argentina then faced Holland for a place in the final. Guided by Johan Cruyff, the Dutch swept the Brazilians aside winning 2–0. The third/fourth place play-off saw Brazil lose 1-0 to Poland. In the final, Holland scored in the first minute from the first penalty awarded in a final but the effervescent Dutch, the best European side to play in any World Cup, couldn't hold out against the hosts, who came back to win 2-1.

1974 World Cup final: Holland 1 West Germany 2, Munich, 77,833

Top scorer in tournament: Gregorz Lato (Poland) 7 goals

WORLD CUP 1978, ARGENTINA

SCOTLAND WORLD CUP SQUAD: Rough *(Partick Thistle)*, Blyth *(Coventry City)*, Jardine *(Rangers)*, Donachie *(Manchester City)*, Forsyth *(Rangers)*, Buchan *(Manchester United)*, McQueen *(Manchester United)*, Kennedy *(Aberdeen)*, Hartford *(Manchester City)*, Gemmill *(Nottingham Forest)*, Macari *(Manchester United)*, Masson *(Derby County)*, Rioch *(Derby County)*, Souness *(Liverpool)*, Dalglish *(Liverpool)*, Burns *(Nottingham Forest)*, Johnstone *(Rangers)*, Jordan *(Manchester United)*, Harper *(Aberdeen)*, Johnston *(West Bromwich Albion)*, Robertson *(Nottingham Forest)*

SCOTLAND 1 PERU 3
Cordoba, 3 June 1978:
Rough, Kennedy, Buchan, Forsyth, Burns, Rioch (Macari), Masson (Gemmill), Hartford, Dalglish, Jordan, Johnston

SCOTLAND 1 IRAN 1
Cordoba, 7 June 1978:
Rough, Jardine, Donachie, Burns, Buchan (Forsyth), Macari, Gemmill, Hartford, Dalglish (Harper), Jordan, Robertson

SCOTLAND 3 HOLLAND 2
Mendoza, 11 June 1978:
Rough, Kennedy, Donachie, Forsyth, Buchan, Rioch, Souness, Gemmill, Hartford, Jordan, Dalglish

The tournament was structured in the same way as in West Germany in 1974. In the last eight, Peru lost all three of their matches, and ten goals without reply, to Brazil, Poland and Argentina. Holland defeated Austria and Italy and drew with West Germany to reach the final. The Dutch, again the best team in the tournament, unluckily lost out to the host nation Argentina, who won 3-1 in extra-time to take their first World Cup.

1978 World Cup final: Argentina 3 Holland 1, Buenos Aires, 77,260

Top scorer in tournament: Mario Kempes (Argentina) 6 goals

WORLD CUP 1982, SPAIN

SCOTLAND WORLD CUP SQUAD: Rough *(Partick Thistle)*, Wood *(Arsenal)*, Leighton *(Aberdeen)*, McGrain *(Celtic)*, F. Gray *(Leeds United)*, Burley *(Ipswich Town)*, Miller *(Aberdeen)*, Narey *(Dundee United)*, Hansen *(Liverpool)*, Evans *(Aston Villa)*, McLeish *(Aberdeen)*, Hartford *(Manchester City)*, Souness *(Liverpool)*, Wark *(Ipswich Town)* Strachan *(Aberdeen)*, Provan *(Celtic)*, Robertson *(Nottingham Forest)*, Dalglish *(Liverpool)*, Archibald *(Tottenham Hotspur)*, Jordan *(AC Milan)*, Sturrock *(Dundee United)*, Brazil *(Ipswich Town)*

SCOTLAND 5 NEW ZEALAND 2
Malaga, 15 June 1982:
Rough, McGrain, Hansen, Evans, Gray, Strachan (Narey), Souness, Wark, Dalglish, Brazil (Archibald), Robertson

SCOTLAND 1 BRAZIL 4
Seville, 18 June 1982:
Rough, Narey, Hansen, Miller, Gray, Strachan (Dalglish), Souness, Wark, Hartford (McLeish), Archibald, Robertson

SCOTLAND 2 USSR 2
Malaga, 22 June 1982:
Rough, Narey, Hansen, Miller, Gray, Strachan (McGrain), Souness, Wark, Archibald, Jordan (Brazil), Robertson

The World Cup finals were expanded to accommodate 24 countries. The first round consisted of six groups of four with the top two from each group moving forward to the next stage which consisted of four groups of three teams. The winners of each group would contest the semi-finals. In the second group stage, the USSR drew with Poland and defeated Belgium. The USSR finished on three points, equal with Poland, but the Poles' superior goal difference gave them the semi-final place. In their three-team group, Brazil beat Argentina but lost 3-2 to Italy in a memorable game. Italy beat Poland in the semi-finals. After a slow start in the final, the Italians defeated the West Germans in fine style.

1982 World Cup final: Italy 3 West Germany 1, Madrid, 90,000

Top scorer in tournament: Paolo Rossi (Italy) 6 goals

WORLD CUP 1986, MEXICO

Scotland World Cup squad: Goram *(Oldham Athletic)*, Leighton *(Aberdeen)*, Rough *(Hibs)*, Albiston *(Manchester United)*, Gough *(Dundee United)*, McLeish *(Aberdeen)*, Malpas *(Dundee United)*, Miller *(Aberdeen)*, Narey *(Dundee United)*, Aitken *(Celtic)*, Bannon *(Dundee United)*, Bett *(Aberdeen)*, McStay *(Celtic)*, Nicol *(Liverpool)*, Souness *(Rangers)*, Strachan *(Manchester United)*, Cooper *(Rangers)*, Archibald *(Barcelona)*, McAvennie *(West Ham United)*, Nicholas *(Arsenal)*, Sharp *(Everton)*, Sturrock *(Dundee United)*

SCOTLAND 0 DENMARK 1
Nezahualcoyotl, 4 June 1986:
Leighton, Gough, Malpas, Souness, McLeish, Miller, Strachan (Bannon), Aitken, Nicol, Nicholas, Sturrock (McAvennie)

SCOTLAND 1 WEST GERMANY 2
Queretaro, 8 June 1986:
Leighton, Gough, Malpas, Souness, Narey, Miller, Strachan, Aitken, Bannon (Cooper), Nicol (McAvennie), Archibald

SCOTLAND 0 URUGUAY 0
Nezahualcoyotl, 13 June 1986:
Leighton, Gough, Albiston, Aitken, Narey, Miller, Strachan, McStay, Sharp, Nicol (Nicholas), Sturrock (Cooper)

Again 24 countries took part with the first round consisting of six groups of four. This time, the top two from each group and the four best third-placed teams moved forward to a 16-team knockout stage. Uruguay lost 1-0 to Argentina while the Danes lost 5-1 to Spain in an incredible match. West Germany beat Morocco 1-0 then, in the quarter-finals, beat the hosts Mexico on penalties after a 0-0 draw. In the semi-finals the Germans defeated France 2-0 to face the Diego Maradona-inspired Argentina in the final. After being 2-0 down the Germans got back to 2-2 but Argentina got the decider in extra-time to win 3-2.

1986 World Cup final: Argentina 3 West Germany 2, Mexico City, 114,590

Top scorer in tournament: Gary Lineker (England) 6 goals

WORLD CUP 1990, ITALY

Scotland World Cup squad: Leighton *(Manchester United)*, Goram *(Hibs)*, Gunn *(Norwich)*, McKimmie *(Aberdeen)*, Malpas *(Dundee United)*, Gough *(Rangers)*, McLeish *(Aberdeen)*, Gillespie *(Liverpool)*, Levein *(Hearts)*, McPherson *(Hearts)*, MacLeod *(Borussia Dortmund)*, Aitken *(Newcastle United)*, Bett *(Aberdeen)*, McStay *(Celtic)*, Collins *(Hibs)*, McCall *(Everton)*, McAllister *(Leicester City)*, Johnston *(Rangers)*, McCoist *(Rangers)*, Durie *(Chelsea)*, McInally *(Bayern Munich)*, Fleck *(Norwich City)*

SCOTLAND 0 COSTA RICA 1
Genoa, 11 June 1990:
Leighton, Gough (McKimmie), Malpas, McPherson, McLeish, Aitken, McCall, McStay, Johnston, McInally, Bett (McCoist)

SCOTLAND 2 SWEDEN 1
Genoa, 16 June 1990:
Leighton, McPherson, Malpas, Aitken, Levein, McLeish, Fleck, MacLeod, Johnston (McCoist), McCall, Durie (McStay)

SCOTLAND 0 BRAZIL 1
Turin, 20 June 1990:
Leighton, McKimmie, Malpas, McPherson, McLeish, MacLeod (Gillespie), Aitken, McStay, Johnston, McCoist (Fleck), McCall

The format for the Italian World Cup was identical to that used in Mexico in 1986. At the 16-team knockout stage, Brazil lost, unluckily, 1-0 to Argentina. Costa Rica were beaten 4-1 by Czechoslovakia. The Argentinians reached the final, a tortuously dull affair, where they lost 1-0 to a West German penalty. The Argentinians had just nine men on the field at the end, having become the first team to have a player sent off in the final. The first offender, Monzon, had subsequently been joined on a red card by Dezotti.

1990 World Cup final: Argentina 0 West Germany 1, Rome, 73,603

Top scorer in tournament: Toto Schillaci (Italy) 6 goals

YEAR BY YEAR SCORES AND GROUP TABLES

1954

Group 3

Austria	1	Scotland	0
Uruguay	2	Czechoslovakia	0
Austria	5	Czechoslovakia	0
Uruguay	7	Scotland	0

	P	W	D	L	F	A	P
Uruguay	2	2	0	0	9	0	4
Austria	2	2	0	0	6	0	4
Czechoslovakia	2	0	0	2	0	7	0
Scotland	2	0	0	2	0	8	0

1958

Group 2

Yugoslavia	1	Scotland	1
France	7	Paraguay	3
Paraguay	3	Scotland	2
Yugoslavia	3	France	2
France	2	Scotland	1
Paraguay	3	Yugoslavia	3

	P	W	D	L	F	A	P
France	3	2	0	1	11	7	4
Yugoslavia	3	1	2	0	7	6	4
Paraguay	3	1	1	1	7	12	3
Scotland	3	0	1	2	4	6	1

1974

Group 2

Brazil	0	Yugoslavia	0
Scotland	2	Zaire	0
Brazil	0	Scotland	0
Yugoslavia	9	Zaire	0
Scotland	1	Yugoslavia	0
Brazil	3	Zaire	0

	P	W	D	L	F	A	P
Yugoslavia	3	1	2	0	10	1	4
Brazil	3	1	2	0	3	0	4
Scotland	3	1	2	0	3	1	4
Zaire	3	0	0	3	0	14	0

1978

Group 4

Peru	3	Scotland	1
Holland	3	Iran	0
Iran	1	Scotland	1
Holland	0	Peru	0
Peru	4	Iran	1
Scotland	3	Holland	2

	P	W	D	L	F	A	P
Peru	3	2	1	0	7	2	5
Holland	3	1	1	1	5	3	3
Scotland	3	1	1	1	5	6	3
Iran	3	0	1	2	2	8	1

1982

Group 6

Brazil	2	USSR	1
Scotland	5	New Zealand	2
Brazil	4	Scotland	1
USSR	3	New Zealand	0
USSR	2	Scotland	2
Brazil	4	New Zealand	0

	P	W	D	L	F	A	P
Brazil	3	3	0	0	10	2	6
USSR	3	1	1	1	6	4	3
Scotland	3	1	1	1	8	8	3
N.–Zealand	3	0	0	3	2	12	0

1986

Group E

Denmark	1	Scotland	0
Uruguay	1	West Germany	1
Denmark	6	Uruguay	1
West Germany	2	Scotland	1
Denmark	2	West Germany	0
Scotland	0	Uruguay	0

	P	W	D	L	F	A	P
Denmark	3	3	0	0	9	1	6
W. Germany	3	1	1	1	3	4	3
Uruguay	3	0	2	1	2	7	2
Scotland	3	0	1	2	1	3	1

1990

Group C

Brazil	2	Sweden	1
Costa Rica	1	Scotland	0
Brazil	1	Costa Rica	0
Scotland	2	Sweden	1
Brazil	1	Scotland	0
Costa Rica	2	Sweden	1

	P	W	D	L	F	A	P
Brazil	3	3	0	0	4	1	6
Costa Rita	3	2	0	1	3	2	4
Scotland	3	1	0	2	2	3	2
Sweden	3	0	0	3	3	6	0

Selected Bibliography

A Scottish Internationalists' Who's Who, 1872-1986, Douglas Lamming, Hutton Press Ltd, North Humberside, 1987

Scotland the Quest for the World Cup, Clive Leatherdale, Two Heads Publishing in association with Desert Island Books, West Sussex, 1994

Photographic Acknowledgements

Cover:
Kenny Dalglish: Colorsport
Lawrie Reilly: © Science & Society Picture Library
Memorabilia: Chris Hall Photography
Billy Bremner: Colorsport

Pages:
Allsport 17, (and Historical Collection) 53 top, (and Michael King) 72, (and Simon Bruty) 76, 78 top, (and Ben Radford) 78 bottom; Colorsport 1, 6-7, 27, 28, 29, 32, 33, 34, 35, 36, 37, 38, 39, 41, 42, 44, 45, 50, 51 bottom, 52, 53 bottom, 59, 60, 61, 62, 63, 64, 65, 67, 69, 70, 71, 73, 74, 75, 79, 82-3, 84, 86, 87, 88-9; © D C Thomson & Co. Ltd 11, 13, 16, 19, 20, 24 top; NMPFT/Science & Society Picture Library 8, 10, 14, 15, 22, 23, 24 bottom, 25; Popperfoto 66; Scottish Daily Record 47.

The memorabilia on the pages of this book are supplied courtesy of The Memorabilia Pack Company.